CompTIA Security+ Practice Tests SY0-501

Practice tests in 4 different formats and 6 cheat sheets to help you pass the CompTIA Security+ exam

Ian Neil

BIRMINGHAM - MUMBAI

CompTIA Security+ Practice Tests SY0-501

Copyright © 2020 Packt Publishing

All rights reserved. No part of this book may be reproduced, stored in a retrieval system, or transmitted in any form or by any means, without the prior written permission of the publisher, except in the case of brief quotations embedded in critical articles or reviews.

Every effort has been made in the preparation of this book to ensure the accuracy of the information presented. However, the information contained in this book is sold without warranty, either express or implied. Neither the author, nor Packt Publishing or its dealers and distributors, will be held liable for any damages caused or alleged to have been caused directly or indirectly by this book.

Packt Publishing has endeavored to provide trademark information about all of the companies and products mentioned in this book by the appropriate use of capitals. However, Packt Publishing cannot guarantee the accuracy of this information.

Commissioning Editor: Vijin Boricha
Acquisition Editor: Rahul Nair
Content Development Editor: Drashti Panchal
Senior Editor: Arun Nadar
Technical Editor: Komal Karne
Copy Editor: Safis Editing
Project Coordinator: Anish Daniel
Proofreader: Safis Editing
Indexer: Manju Arasan
Production Designer: Alishon Mendonca

First published: January 2020

Production reference: 2170920

Published by Packt Publishing Ltd.
Livery Place
35 Livery Street
Birmingham
B3 2PB, UK.

ISBN 978-1-83882-888-2

www.packt.com

I am dedicating this book to all of those people who strive to improve their careers by seeking knowledge or certification, especially those individuals whose careers depend on certification, ranging from those with no prior knowledge to the IT professional.

Packt.com

Subscribe to our online digital library for full access to over 7,000 books and videos, as well as industry leading tools to help you plan your personal development and advance your career. For more information, please visit our website.

Why subscribe?

- Spend less time learning and more time coding with practical eBooks and Videos from over 4,000 industry professionals

- Improve your learning with Skill Plans built especially for you

- Get a free eBook or video every month

- Fully searchable for easy access to vital information

- Copy and paste, print, and bookmark content

Did you know that Packt offers eBook versions of every book published, with PDF and ePub files available? You can upgrade to the eBook version at www.packt.com and as a print book customer, you are entitled to a discount on the eBook copy. Get in touch with us at customercare@packtpub.com for more details.

At www.packt.com, you can also read a collection of free technical articles, sign up for a range of free newsletters, and receive exclusive discounts and offers on Packt books and eBooks.

Contributors

About the author

Ian Neil is one of the world's top trainers of Security+ 501, who has the ability to break down information into manageable chunks helping no background knowledge. Ian was a finalist of the Learning and Performance Institute Trainer of the Year Awards. He has worked for the US Army in Europe and designed a Security+ course that catered to people from all backgrounds and not just the IT professional, with an extremely successful pass rate. He was instrumental in helping Microsoft get their office in Bucharest off the ground, where he won a recognition award for being one of their top trainers. Ian is an MCT, MCSE, A+, Network+, Security+, CASP, and RESILIA practitioner who over the past 20 years has worked with high-end training providers.

I acknowledge the support I have had from Drashti Panchal, Rahul Nair, and Komal Karne in producing this book.

About the reviewers

Philip Brooker is an IT security consultant based in the United Kingdom who works with small, medium, and large enterprises in the private sector. Formerly, he worked as an IT systems administrator and project engineer. With over a decade of IT experience, Philip has achieved numerous industry certifications, including, of course, CompTIA Security+.

> *I would like to thank my partner, Jessica, and my son, Oliver, without whom none of my work would be possible. I will always be grateful for their continued love and support. And a big thank you to both Packt and the author, without whom there would be no book!*

Francisco Gaspar is an engineer by training, cyber security architect by trade, and a team player by nature.

First and foremost, he is a geek, as he breathes technology. He has always had a special interest in robotics and AI and, more recently, has developed an interest in quantum computing. He endeavors to be a cyber security evangelist whenever he has the opportunity.

He has mentored in a program that helps people retrain to become programmers and, for the last 3 years, he has lived in Dublin, where he has been involved as a mentor in launching start-ups in a program called UpStart, at Trinity College, Dublin. This program is sponsored by CitiBank.

His most well-known publication/appearance was in TED, where he has done a TED talk on cyber security.

Packt is searching for authors like you

If you're interested in becoming an author for Packt, please visit `authors.packtpub.com` and apply today. We have worked with thousands of developers and tech professionals, just like you, to help them share their insight with the global tech community. You can make a general application, apply for a specific hot topic that we are recruiting an author for, or submit your own idea.

Table of Contents

Preface

CompTIA Security+ is a worldwide certification that establishes the fundamental knowledge required to perform core security functions and pursue an IT security career. This book consists of practice tests in four different formats to prepare you for becoming certified.

Who this book is for

Individuals who will benefit from this book include military personnel and DOD civilians who require this certification for their job role. It is a great resource for those students who wish to gain employment/a degree in cyber security or who are preparing to gain a baseline before embarking on the CISSP certification.

What this book covers

Chapter 1, *Threats, Attacks, and Vulnerabilities Practice Tests*, contains four different format practice tests, including a mock exam.

Chapter 2, *Technologies and Tools Practice Tests*, contains four different format practice tests, including a mock exam.

Chapter 3, *Architecture and Design Practice Tests*, contains four different format practice tests, including a mock exam.

Chapter 4, *Identity and Access Management Practice Tests*, contains four different format practice tests, including a mock exam.

Chapter 5, *Cryptography and PKI Practice Tests*, contains four different format practice tests, including a mock exam.

Chapter 6, *Risk Management*, contains four different format practice tests, including a mock exam.

To get the most out of this book

Students using this book should have completed a course of instruction or read a CompTIA study guide for the CompTIA Security+ 501 exam. A book that complements this practice test book is the *CompTIA Security+ Certification Guide* (https://www.packtpub.com/in/networking-and-servers/comptia-security-certification-guide), written by Ian Neil.

Get in touch

Feedback from our readers is always welcome.

General feedback: If you have questions about any aspect of this book, mention the book title in the subject of your message and email us at customercare@packtpub.com.

Errata: Although we have taken every care to ensure the accuracy of our content, mistakes do happen. If you have found a mistake in this book, we would be grateful if you would report this to us. Please visit www.packtpub.com/support/errata, selecting your book, clicking on the Errata Submission Form link, and entering the details.

Piracy: If you come across any illegal copies of our works in any form on the internet, we would be grateful if you would provide us with the location address or website name. Please contact us at copyright@packt.com with a link to the material.

If you are interested in becoming an author: If there is a topic that you have expertise in, and you are interested in either writing or contributing to a book, please visit authors.packtpub.com.

Reviews

Please leave a review. Once you have read and used this book, why not leave a review on the site that you purchased it from? Potential readers can then see and use your unbiased opinion to make purchase decisions, we at Packt can understand what you think about our products, and our authors can see your feedback on their book. Thank you!

For more information about Packt, please visit packt.com.

1
Threats, Attacks, and Vulnerabilities Practice Tests

One of the most crucial areas that a security professional needs to have knowledge about is the type of attacks that there are and the ways that these attacks can be mitigated so that your company is less vulnerable to attacks. The CompTIA exam breaks this examination topic into different areas.

The first area we look at is the types of malware that exist, such as basic viruses, worms, trojans, ransomware, adware, spyware, rootkits, keyloggers, logic bombs, and backdoor.

Next, we will compare and contrast the different types of attacks. This area is immense. We will also look at the different types of social engineering attacks, where the individual is seen as the weak link that the attacker will try to exploit. These attacks range from phishing, spear phishing, whaling, vishing, tailgating, impersonating, dumpster diving, shoulder surfing, hoaxes, and watering-hole attacks. IT professionals need to be familiar with social engineering attacks such as authority, intimidation, consensus, and urgency.

We are also going to look at application service attacks, such as DoS, DDoS, man-in-the-middle, buffer overflow, integer overflow, SQL injection, XSS, XSRF, amplification, DNS poisoning, ARP poisoning, domain hijacking, zero-day virus, replay, and pass-the-hash attacks. We will also be looking at hijacking and related attacks, such as clickjacking, session hijacking, typosquatting, and driver manipulation. We will also look at wireless attacks, ranging from evil twin, rogue access point, jamming, WPS, bluejacking, bluesnarfing, RFID, NFC, and disassociation. No exam would be complete without cryptographic attacks, such as birthday, rainbow-table, dictionary, brute-force, collision, and downgrade attacks.

You need to know and identify the motivation of the threat actors that you will face, and these range from the script kiddie with little knowledge to the politically motivated hacktivist, nation-states, advanced persistent threats, competitors, and the most dangerous malicious insider threat. Every security professional will need to know about penetration tests that can be intrusive and cause damage, such as the black, white, and gray box penetration testers to the non-credentialed, credentialed, false positive, and real time monitoring. We need to look at the impact of vulnerabilities, such as race conditions, end-of-life systems, lack of vendor support, default configurations, untrained users, handling and setting up errors, undocumented assets, zero-day viruses, and key management.

This publication is not a study guide, but gives you additional examination revision material so that your knowledge base can be at its highest when you take the test. Everyone has different ways of learning, and hopefully, with four different formats, everyone should be catered for.

Before you begin each set of tests, you need to keep a sheet of paper so that areas that you get wrong or are guessing at are written down to help identify the weak areas that you need to revise before testing.

After the test, there is a *Cheat Sheet* section, containing a shortened version of the most relevant information that you need to know to pass this test.

Practice Test 1 – Open Questions – Threats, Attacks, and Vulnerabilities

Start off by answering the questions that you have the knowledge base to answer, then on a separate list write down the questions that you do not know the answers to, because you need to revise those areas before testing:

1. What type of virus produces a different hash as it replicates through your network?

2. What type of attack can use a hidden password that has been in place since the application was installed?

3. What type of attack involves an agent attacking a high-level executive calling them on a telephone and leaving a voicemail?

4. What type of attack involves a huge fireman arriving in the reception area of your company and you letting him into your server room?

5. What type of attack involves downloading a performance-enhancing computer program that says that I have 20,000 exploits and that I should purchase the full version of the product to remove them?

6. What type of attack collects passwords from your computer and sends them back to the hacker who then uses these passwords to gain access to your computer system?

7. What type of attack cannot be detected by a NIPS, NIDS, firewall, or a SIEM system, but can only be detected by using baselines?

8. An employee leaves the company, then three months later, files are deleted from a file server, even though it has been isolated from the network. On investigation, it was found that the damage was caused by a script being launched. What type of attack was carried out?

9. What type of attack is a stealth attack that tracks your internet habits and usage?

10. What type of attack uses multiple popups as its attack vector?

11. What type of attack infects a well-known, trusted website where the users do not suspect anything?

12. What type of attack is launched against a manager using email as its attack medium?

13. What type of attack is launched against managers using email as its attack medium?

14. A company is employing a third party to collect all of its shredded waste that will then be taken to a remote site and incinerated. What type of attack does this prevent?

15. What type of attack is launched when you receive an email from the CEO threatening you with disciplinary action if you do not complete a form that was requested earlier by the human resources department (you don't remember the earlier correspondence)?

16. You have just started working at the reception desk of a multinational corporation. During your induction period, one of the middle managers asks your coworker for some information. You are not too sure if he is entitled to that information. The next day, when your coworker has gone to lunch, the middle manager arrives asking you for the same information, this time updated a little. You don't want to be seen as different from other employees, and so you give him the information. What type of attack has just been launched?

17. The CEO has received an email asking him to click on a link and carry out an action so that his salary information can be updated, as the company is moving to a new financial system. What type of attack has just been launched?

18. What type of attack can be launched using HTML tags and/or JavaScript?

19. When might an intrusive scan be used, and could it cause any damage to the system?

20. Five seconds after connecting to the company's wireless network, the sessions drop. What type of wireless attack have I been the victim of?

21. A hacker has managed to gain access to my Bluetooth phone and has been texting all of my friends, announcing that I am going to get married next year. This information is false. What type of attack has just been carried out?

22. A hacker has managed to gain access to my Bluetooth phone and has been able to steal my contact information. What type of attack has been carried out?

23. What type of attack is an interception attack where the data has been replayed immediately?

24. What type of attack is an interception attack where the data has been replayed at a later date?

25. What types of attack might use port 1900 and port 5000? Name two.

26. I receive a call from my bank saying that they need to move my account to an interest-bearing account, and ask me to go through the application process. They ask me for my account details and direct me to choose a new online password. They need my old password for account verification. What type of attack has been carried out?

27. In the morning, I swipe my card and open the door to the main offices. I am about to close the door when I see a young lady struggling with a big box, and so I keep the door open for her. What type of attack has just occurred?

28. The customer service desk receives a call from Frank, who says he is from the IT help desk. He says there is a glitch in the system, so they are having to change everyone's passwords. I change my password and ask Helen from the HR department how long Frank has been working for the company. She says that she is not aware of someone called Frank who works at the help desk. What type of attack has just occurred?

29. What type of attack is it when a group of infected computers attacks another computer to render it unusable?

30. I went to the ATM to withdraw some cash to purchase a new pair of shoes from a local market stall that only accepts cash. I was unaware that the person standing behind me had taken his cell phone out and was using the video to record my transaction. What type of attack has been carried out?

31. An attacker has inserted too much data into a data field on a web form causing it to crash. What type of attack has just occurred?

32. What type of attack uses the phrase 1=1? What are the two best solutions to prevent this attack?

33. My website traffic is being controlled by a load balancer that is ensuring that each web request is going to the least-utilized host. A DDoS attack is now being launched against the company websites. What is the best way to deal with this attack? Will the load balancer cope?

34. When I go to my local coffee shop, I am given the wireless network SSID and access code so I can use the internet while drinking coffee. When I sit down at my table, I notice that the SSID comes up, and when I connect to the wireless network, I am not asked for a password. What type of attack has just occurred?

35. How can I protect my network from someone who wants to connect a rogue access point to it?

36. What type of attack interferes with my wireless network?

37. My laptop had a virus, so I reinstalled the operating system and the virus came back. What type of attack is causing this?

38. My domain controller uses NTLM authentication. What type of attack makes it vulnerable?

39. Someone goes to the dark web and purchases a program that he can modify to carry out an attack. What type of threat actor is the attacker?

40. An attacker has just carried out an attack rendering a website unusable. When he has finished the attack, he then has to rush off, as he is going to attend a political rally. What type of threat actor is he?

41. What is the most difficult threat actor to detect and why?

42. What type of threat actor will try to steal your trade secrets so that they can manufacture your new product and get it to market before you can?

43. An attacker has managed to gain access to your corporate network through a host that was not fully patched. Once he gained access to that host, he then launched an attack on your SQL database server so that he could steal your customer's credit card details. What type of technique did the attacker adopt?

44. Your company has contracted a third party to carry out penetration testing to identify any weaknesses in your system, as you recently had it upgraded. You have given them no information except a small diagram of a remote part of your network. What type of penetration test is being carried out?

45. Why would a white-box penetration tester who knows everything about your network and applications adopt a technique called fuzzing when testing a new application?

46. How much information should a black-box penetration tester be given and what would be the first technique that he should adopt?

47. How do penetration testing and vulnerability scanning differ?

48. If I had an end-of-life controller for my HVAC system, but could not afford to replace it for another four months, how might I mitigate the risk that it poses?

49. You are the **Chief Information Security Officer** (**CISO**) for a large multinational corporation and you are going to write a policy for the website developer to control any errors that come from the website. How will you describe the errors that the users receive and those errors that the IT support team receives?

50. You have an older monitoring system that is not detecting any new vulnerabilities, but the security team informs you that data has been exfiltrated. What is it called when the monitoring system is not detecting attacks?

51. Your security team has informed you that the CPU usage on the SQL server is running at 100%. Which vulnerability is it suffering from and how can you mitigate it?

52. What type of attack launches directed IP broadcasts to the border router where the victim is overloaded with the resulting ping replies? What can you do to mitigate this attack?

53. What type of attack redirects you from a legitimate website and sends you to a fraudulent website?

54. What is the purpose of DNSSEC, what records does it produce, and what type of attack does it prevent?

55. What type of attack involves your cookies being copied onto a different computer to launch an attack?

56. When would a typosquatting attack be performed?

57. A hacker has gone to the dark web and has obtained a 690-GB rainbow table. What are they intending to do with this table and what is the table comprised of?

58. What is the best way to avoid someone cracking your password if they intend to use a dictionary attack as the attack vector? Name two examples.

59. What is the purpose of a brute-force attack and what is the only way to prevent it?

60. What can I do to stop users in my company from storing duplicate passwords and at the same time slow down brute-force attacks?

Practice Test 2 – Fill The Gaps – Threats, Attacks, and Vulnerabilities

Fill-the-gaps questions really test your knowledge base, and can be quite vague at times. In the CompTIA Security+ examination, some of the test questions can also be quite vague, hence the value of this section.

Complete the answers that you can, then make a list of those topics that you are getting wrong, as you need to revise these areas before you take the test. Best of luck.

In the following questions, fill in the gaps to make the statement. Each underlined section of the sentence represents one word—for example, _____ means that one word is missing; _____ _____ means that two words are missing:

1. A _____ _____ attack is where an attacker gains the same level of authorization as the administrator.

2. _____ is wireless authentication that starts off by inserting a password, meaning that you only need to press a button to gain access to the wireless network.

3. _____ _____ is where an attacker will ring up a help desk and ask them to reset the password for a user account.

4. A _____ is where an attacker will ask you to look into the `Windows\System32` folder to find an icon, such as a bear. If you find this icon, they will then ask you to delete the bear, as it is a virus. But when you do this, you will, in fact, delete a system file.

5. XSS targets _____, while remote exploits target _____ _____ .

6. Digital signatures are susceptible to a _____ _____, a hash-collision attack.

7. A _____ attack is an interception attack where the data is forwarded at a later time and can be prevented by using Kerberos authentication that uses updated sequence numbers and timestamps.

8. An auditor discovers that 50 new desktops have not been hardened properly, and puts it down to the fact that _____ _____ had not been implemented early in the deployment.

9. _____ and _____ are both used for driver manipulation.

10. My airplane was delayed and my free time on the wireless captive portal expired. I can use _____ _____ to bypass the captive portal for another session of free wireless access.

11. A ___-_____ vulnerability scan can find only missing patches.

12. A _____ vulnerability scan has the ability to audit files and find account vulnerabilities.

13. A CEO instructs the finance team to urgently send payment to ABC Limited just before he boards an aircraft on a transatlantic flight. This is an example of a social engineering _____ and a _____ attack.

14. An _____-_____ vulnerability scan will not cause damage to the computer system.

15. _____ _____ _____ is a wireless payment system that only works from close range.

16. An HVAC system that is no longer supported by the manufacturer is known as _____ of ___.

17. A _____ _____ is where a monitoring system tells me that an exploit has been found on the system, but when a manual inspection is done, nothing is found.

18. A _____virus accesses a computer system by using a password that has been there since the installation of the application.

19. _____ _____is where an attacker will visit a company's website and social media websites to collect information about the company.

20. A _____ _____ can be used to stop data-processing emissions being intercepted by a third party.

21. Changing the _____ _____ and preventing IoT devices from directly accessing the _____ will help protect home networks from attacks.

22. When a system has come to the end of its life, the vendor will have a lack of _____ _____.

23. _____ _____ threat actors have a level of sophistication and provide advanced persistent threats.

24. _____ _____ can cause your internet bandwidth to be reduced and your server disk space to decrease.

25. _____ is the most insecure method of wireless security and should never be used, as it can be easily attacked.

26. _____ _____ threat actors are motivated by profits and may use blackmail.

27. _____ _____ _____ can be sourced from publicly available intelligence sources.

28. _____ _____ prevents SQL injection, buffer overflow, and integer overflow attacks.

29. A company keeps the keys to all of the offices in the reception area and the workers sign the keys in and out each day. This is known as ____ _____, and it prevents people from taking the keys home with them.

30. The policy of a company is to change the _____ _____ of any new device that they purchase to ensure that it is more secure.

31. _____ _____ suites are where the key size is less than 1024 bits, and should be avoided.

32. The Stuxnet virus is an example of a _____ threat as it infected a computer system for about two years before it was discovered.

33. _____-_____ is the strongest form of wireless security.

34. _____ _____ is what a pen tester will carry out first, based on the information they have.

35. A store had small devices stolen over the last three months. They rolled out _____ to prevent the small devices from leaving the store undetected.

36. Using SSL instead of TLS for data in transit could lead to a POODLE attack that is known as a _____ attack.

37. To protect data in transit, you should use encryption where plaintext is changed to _____.

38. An attacker will try and log into your control panel to launch a _____ _____ attack.

39. A ___-__-____-_____ attack is where a previously installed trojan intercepts your online banking transactions without changing the bank's URL.

40. Both smurf attacks and DDoS attacks are known as _____ attacks.

41. _____ _____ password attacks can detect every available combination of characters and can be stopped by using an account lockout or by salting the password using bcrypt or PBKDF2.

42. _____-____ _____ _____attack is where a user is logged into a legitimate website and clicks on a link where an embedded program is located. This is also known as a one-click attack, XRSF, or CSRF.

43. A _____ attack uses a legitimate website with links—for example, a Like button, a Share button, a free trial, or an Isn't This Funny? link.

44. A ____ _____ is where two threads access the same data at the same time and either cause the computer to crash or give an illegal operation error.

45. _____ _____ is where an arithmetic calculation exceeds the maximum size an application can accept. It can be mitigated by using input validation.

46. _____ prevents duplicate passwords from being stored and slows down brute-force attacks.

47. _____ _____ on your network will not be patched and could be used for pivoting as they become vulnerable.

48. _____ _____ could inadvertently violate security policies and become vulnerable to a cybercrime or phishing attack.

49. _____ _____ is where proprietary code is tested by a consultant for security flaws.

50. _____ _____ of failure is where one person, device, or service could cause damage to the company's systems if it failed.

Practice Test 3 – Drag and Drops – Threats, Attacks, and Vulnerabilities

I suggest using two different-colored pens: blue or black for answers that are easy for you to identify and a red or different-colored pen for answers that you are unsure of. This way, you can identify your strong and weak areas.

Place the answers into the relevant answer boxes in the following table, starting with the answers that you can easily identify. Make a list of those that you cannot answer on your first time through, as you need to revise those areas. Then use logic to answer the remaining questions.

Insert the phrases at the end of this section into the appropriate answer boxes in the following table. Each phrase can only be used once:

Description	Answer
The trial software found exploits, but you need to buy the full package	
More data is inserted into an application than expected	
The reason why we shred and burn data is to prevent ...	
Someone standing behind you records your ATM transaction by using a smartphone	
A USB drive plugged into the back of your desktop logs keystrokes	
This generates multiple popups	
You have reinstalled the operating system, but this virus is still there	
An attack on the CEO or a high-level executive	
Someone willing to steal your trade secrets	
No knowledge or information is given to you	
Prevents pass-the-hash attacks	
An untraceable virus	
May cause harm to your system	
An attack on everyone using a popular trusted website	
Complete wireless payment transactions	
Obtains a program from the dark web	
Redirects the user to a fraudulent website	

Listening to a conversation	
The first stage after purchasing an IoT device, change the ...	
CPU running at 100% is a sign of ...	
An email sent to the Board of Directors	
Purchasing fake software from a website	
An attack using the phrase 1=1	
Hacktivist motivation	
Prevents SQL injection, buffer overflow, and integer overflow	

Use the following options to fill in the blank boxes in the preceding table:

Black-box pen tester	Watering-hole attack	Hoax	Ransomware	Script kiddie
DNS poisoning	SQL injection	Near field communication	Political cause	Buffer overflow
Input validation	Spear phishing	Passive reconnaissance	Dumpster diving	Resource exhaustion
Shoulder surfing	Keylogger	Default configuration	Adware	Rootkit
Whaling	Competitor	Kerberos	Zero-day virus	Intrusive scan

Practice Test 4 – Mock Exam 1

Start off the mock exam with a clean sheet of paper and note down the questions that you cannot answer or are guessing at, because you need to revise those areas. When you take this test, follow these instructions:

DO:

- Read the questions carefully; do not scan. Draw diagrams on questions you are unsure of.
- Rule out the wrong answers to leave the correct answer.
- When you narrow the answers down to two possible answers, you have a 50–50 chance of being right. Read the question again and look for the finer details that will give one of those options a 60–40 chance of being right.
- Flag up for review (in the top-right of the screen) the questions that you don't like. Do not answer them, as the review screen will show those items in red. Don't waste time trying to work them out at this stage.

- Before ending your review, go down the columns from left to right and ensure that all questions have an answer.
- At the end, check all of the questions' answers and finish the exam.

DON'T:

- Scan through the questions, especially if English is your first language
- Second-guess yourself
- Change answers
- Reread the whole exam if you have spare time

Answer the following questions:

1. You are the **Chief Information Security Officer** (**CISO**), and have been invited to meet with the board of directors at their monthly meeting. In that meeting, the CEO states that someone called Joe Hopkins from the help desk has been calling him and some of the board members to help reset their passwords as the old passwords were too insecure. The financial director found this very strange as this Joe Hopkins is not on the payroll. Which of the following is the BEST answer for what has been discovered?

> a. Social engineering.
> b. Spear phishing.
> c. Vishing attack.
> d. Password cracking.
> e. Phishing.
> f. Replay.

2. You are the cybersecurity administrator for a large company that has offices in Stuttgart. The SIEM system alerts you that files are being deleted on file server FS001. The cyber administrator cannot find any remote connection to the file server. He then quarantines the file server from the network. The deletion of the files is still in progress. The forensics team discovers that a script was placed there by Dave Lloyd, who had left the company exactly four weeks ago. Which of the following BEST describes the actions of Dave Lloyd?

> a. Dave Lloyd installed a RAT into the file server and is actively removing files.
> b. Dave Lloyd placed a logic bomb on the file server to delete the files once he had gone so that he was not a suspect.
> c. Dave Lloyd installed ransomware to encrypt the customers' critical files.
> d. Dave Lloyd connected through a VPN connection and remotely deleted files.

3. Following an annual penetration test, the chief information security officer notices in the final report that all of the company's domain controllers are vulnerable to a pass-the-hash attack. Which of the following actions should the company take to mitigate the risk (choose TWO)?

       a. Enable CHAP.
       b. Disable CHAP.
       c. Disable NTLM.
       d. Disable MD5.
       e. Enable Kerberos.
       f. Disable PAP.

4. The new interns in the IT team are having a heated discussion on the differences between cross-site scripting and cross-site reverse forgery vulnerabilities. They have four different scenarios and want you as the chief information security officer to provide a solution. Which of the following will you select?

       a. Cross-site reverse forgery does not need the victim to be authenticated by a domain controller.
       b. Cross-site scripting needs the attacker to be authenticated by the domain controller.
       c. Cross-site scripting does not need the victim to be authenticated by the trusted server.
       d. Cross-site reverse forgery needs the victim to be authenticated by the trusted server.

5. A well-known hacker called Mark Birch has been detained by the local police. When they searched his home, they found various pieces of information about your company on a large whiteboard. The information has been obtained from a social media website, such as Facebook and LinkedIn. It has details about the company's hierarchy, the executives, administrators, and help-desk staff. Which of the following BEST describes the type of attack he has carried out?

       a. White-box testing.
       b. Passive reconnaissance.
       c. Black-box testing.
       d. Initial exploitation.
       e. Gray-box testing.
       g. Intrusive scanning.

6. You are a cybersecurity analyst working for the local police department because of an increase in crime being carried out by the vulnerabilities of IoT devices. You are running a one-hour session to advise homeowners due to vulnerabilities:

- The attack vector of MFD used at home
- Control of passwords with IoT devices
- How to ensure that no attacks can be carried out through IoT devices

Which of the following BEST meets with the preceding objectives (choose THREE)?

a. Prevent IoT devices connecting directly to the internet.
b. Ensure that you have faster bandwidth to enable the smooth running of IoT devices.
c. MFD devices are attacked via their spooler.
d. MFD devices are attacked via their network interface.
e. Change the default username and password one day after device activation, as it takes that long to be established.
f. Change the default username and password immediately.

7. You are the chief information security officer for a large multinational corporation that has offices in Hong Kong, London, Paris, and New York. The New York office has 100 employees, The Hong Kong office has five employees, Paris has four employees, and London has the most, with 10,000 employees. You have purchased a small company based in Alaska that has four people. They have been using weak passwords. Which of the following is a compensating control that was adopted to BEST mitigate the risk of using weak passwords?

a. Use a password history with a value of 3.
b. Implement time-based one-time passwords.
c. Increase the password history to a value of 20.
d. Set the account lockout to a value of 1.
e. Set the password expiry to three days.

8. What type of attack is a padding oracle on downgrading legacy encryption attack (Choose TWO)?

a. IV attack.
b. Replay attack.
c. Man-in-the-middle attack.
d. TLS 1.0 with electronic-code book.
e. SSL 3.0 with chain-block cipher.

9. The cybersecurity team have set up a honeypot to track the attack vector of a newly released malware. As they review the virus, they notice that the hash value of the malware changes from host to host. Which of the following types of malware has been detected?

    a. Virus.
    b. RAT.
    c. Worm.
    d. Logic bomb.
    e. Polymorphic virus.

10. The cybersecurity team have looked at the latest trends and have identified that there has been an increase in brute-force attacks. Which of the following is a random value that can be appended to the stored password to make it more difficult for a brute-force password attack to be carried out (choose TWO)?

    a. Obfuscation.
    b. Nonce.
    c. Key stretching.
    d. Salting.

11. There has been a spate of DNS-poisoning attacks and your company wants to make itself resilient against these attacks. Your company wants to encrypt the DNS traffic by using DNSSEC. Once you have signed the zone, what record is created for each host?

    a. CNAME.
    b. SPF.
    c. RRSIG.
    d. MX.
    e. PTR.

12. A security administrator discovers that an attacker used a compromised host as a platform for launching attacks deeper into a company's network. What terminology BEST describes the use of the compromised host?

    a. Brute force.
    b. Active reconnaissance.
    c. Pivoting.
    d. Passing point.

13. At what stage of the SDLC are computer systems no longer supported by the original vendor?

    a. Sandboxing.
    b. End-of-life systems.

c. Resource exhaustion.

d. System sprawl.

14. Company A has just developed a bespoke system for booking airline tickets. What is it called if a freelance coding specialist tests it for security flaws?

    a. Code review.

    b. Static-code review.

    c. Regression testing.

    d. Dynamic-code review.

15. You are the security administrator for an airline company that suffered a loss of availability of their systems last month. Which of the following attacks would MOST LIKELY affect the availability of your IT systems?

    a. Spear phishing.

    b. Replay.

    c. Man-in-the-middle.

    d. DoS.

16. You are a lecturer in a college and you need to deliver a session on salting passwords. What are the two main reasons you would salt passwords?

    a. To slow down brute-force attacks.

    b. To make access to the password slower.

    c. To prevent duplicate passwords from being stored.

    d. To stop simple passwords from being used.

17. An auditor is carrying out an annual inspection of a SCADA network and finds that the **programmable logic controllers** (**PLCs**) have not been updated since last year. Upon further investigation, it is discovered that the company manufacturing these PLCs has gone into liquidation, making these controls end-of-life systems. The manufacturer is currently looking for another company to make an upgraded PLC. Which of the following recommendations should the auditor make to the management team to mitigate the risk in the short term?

    a. Remove the PLCs from the manufacturing infrastructure.

    b. Produce their own updated PLCs for the firmware.

    c. Set up a SIEM system for real-time monitoring of the SCADA system.

    d. Place the PLCs in a VLAN.

18. The security administrator has identified an unknown vulnerability on an application that is used infrequently. They have isolated the application and gathered information to send to the vendor so that a patch can be produced. Once the company receives a patch for the application, what is the best way for the company to test the application before rolling it out into production?

> a. Obfuscation.
> b. VLAN.
> c. Regression testing.
> d. Sandboxing.

19. What is it called when a user has exploited an IT system so that he has obtained access to all files on the file server?

> a. Remote exploit.
> b. Zero-day exploit.
> c. Privilege escalation.
> d. Pivoting.

20. Which of the following is an email-based attack on all members of the sales team?

> a. Phishing.
> b. Vishing.
> c. Spear phishing.
> d. Pharming.

21. An attacker tries to target a high-level executive, but unfortunately has to leave a voicemail as they did not answer the telephone. What was the intended attack and what attack was eventually was used (choose all that apply)?

> a. Whaling.
> b. Vishing.
> c. Phishing.
> d. Spear phishing.

22. You are carrying out annual training for your company and need to put a PowerPoint slide together for the symptoms of a backdoor virus. Which three bullet points will you include in the slide? Each provides part of the explanation of a backdoor virus.

> a. Passwords may have been there a long time.
> b. You must click on several items.
> c. Can be included in an email attachment.

d. Files open quicker than before.

e. You can only get infected through a link on a webpage.

23. Which of the following commands can be used to create a buffer overflow (choose all that apply)?

a. `var char`.

b. `strcpy`.

c. `var data`.

d. `strcat`.

24. You are the security administrator for a multinational corporation and the development team have asked your advice as to how BEST to prevent SQL injection, integer overflow, and buffer overflow attacks. Which of the following should you advise them to use?

a. Input validation.

b. A host-based firewall with advanced security.

c. `strcpy`.

d. Hashing.

25. Your company is opening up a new data center in Galway in Ireland where you have installed the server farm, and now a construction company has come in to put a six-foot mantrap into the entrance. What the main two reasons why this mantrap has been installed?

a. To prevent theft.

b. To prevent tailgating.

c. To prevent unauthorized personnel gaining access to the data center.

d. To allow faster access to the facility.

26. Which of the following devices can prevent unauthorized access to the network and prevent attacks from unknown sources?

a. Router.

b. Load balancer.

c. Web-security gateway.

d. UTM.

27. You are the cybersecurity analyst for a large corporation, and have been investigating recent incidents. You found an attacker who seems to be trying to post political messages on your company website. Which of the following BEST describes this threat actor?

a. Organized crime.

b. Script kiddie.

    c. Hacktivist.
    d. APT.
    e. Malicious insider.
    f. Nation state.

28. A security administrator wants to audit a web application to determine whether default accounts are being used. What technique is being used to carry this task out?

    a. Social engineering.
    b. Banner grabbing.
    c. Protocol analyzer.
    d. Netcat (nc).

29. You are the CISO for a large financial institution. You are setting up an annual contract with a third-party company who will take the data away for shredding and pulping. What type of attack are you preventing?

    a. Social engineering.
    b. Dumpster diving.
    c. Watering-hole attack.
    d. Smurf attack.
    e. Replay attack.

30. You are the chief information security officer for a large corporation and you have been informed that the forms on the company's website are passing unsanitized values to the backend ticketing system. Which of the following types of attack has been carried out?

    a. Input validation.
    b. Buffer overflow.
    c. XSS attack.
    d. Replay attack.
    e. SQL injection.
    f. Integer overflow.

31. Company A are using a third party to perform a pen test against the company's network. No information has been given to the company prior to their visit. As the pen testers are about to start testing, one of the ladies from the network gives them a floor plan showing all of the network points. Which type of pen testing is being carried out?

    a. Gray box.
    b. White box.
    c. Intrusive scan.
    d. Black box.

32. You are the cybersecurity analyst for a large corporation, and have been analyzing various log files on the external firewall. You notice the following:
SELECT* from Customers, Orders, Bank Account Number, 1=1.

Which of the following types of attack is being carried out?

     a. Buffer overflow.
     b. Social engineering.
     c. Customer services are printing off a list of all customers.
     d. SQL injection.
     e. Smurf.

33. A black-box pen tester has crashed the company's main systems. Which type of scan have they been using?

     a. Intrusive scan.
     b. Vulnerability scan.
     c. Non-credentialed.
     d. Application scan.

34. You are an employee working in the finance department, and have just received an email from the **Chief Financial Officer** (**CFO**) instructing you to pay $3,000 immediately to a vendor before critical services are cut. The vendor's invoice is attached for ease of reference. Which of the following BEST describes the type of attack being used (choose TWO)?

     a. Impersonating.
     b. Shoulder surfing.
     c. Consensus/social proof.
     d. Authority.
     e. Urgency.

35. A payroll department has contacted the security team regarding a problem with the transfer of the payroll that was submitted to the bank. The payroll system log files revealed the following entries:
September 1, 2020, August Payroll File created – File transferred to the bank
October 1, 2020, September Payroll File created – File transferred to the bank
November 1, 2020, October Payroll File created – Transfer failed
November 2, 2020, October Payroll File created – File transferred to the bank
Which of the following explains why the file transfer failed?

     a. The file hashed changed while in transit.
     b. The file was transferred to the wrong destination.

c. The file was corrupted while in transit.

d. The bank refused the transfer.

36. During a routine review of firewall log reports, a security technician discovers multiple successful logins for users during unusual hours. The technician contacts the network administrator, who confirms that the logins were not related to the administrator's activities. Which of the following is the MOST likely reason for these logins?

a. Firewall maintenance service windows were scheduled.

b. Default credentials were still in place.

c. The entries in the log were caused by the file-integrity monitoring system.

d. A blue team was conducting a penetration test on the firewall.

37. A security analyst is assigned to perform a penetration test for one of the company's clients. During the scope discussion, the analyst is notified that the client is not going to share any information related to the environment to be tested. Which of the following BEST identifies this type of penetration testing?

a. Black box.

b. White box.

c. Gray box.

d. Blue teaming.

38. Company emails have been intercepted and altered in transit. The security administrator needs to implement a solution that provides both email integrity and nonrepudiation. Which of the following should he use?

a. OAuth.

b. Kerberos.

c. S/MIME.

d. TLS.

39. Which of the following is an example of resource exhaustion?

a. A penetration tester requests every available IP address from a DHCP server.

b. An SQL injection attack returns confidential data back to the browser.

c. Server CPU utilization peaks at 100% during the reboot process.

d. System requirements for a new software package recommend having 12 GB of RAM, but only 8 GB are available.

40. A security scanner lists security discrepancies that are not present when the system is manually inspected. Which of the following is the MOST likely reason for this?

      a. Credentialed scan.
      b. Fail-acceptance rate.
      c. False positives.
      d. False negatives.

41. Which of the following methods minimizes the use of a system interaction when conducting a vulnerability scan?

      a. Stopping the firewall service.
      b. Running a credentialed scan first thing in the morning.
      c. Conducting the assessment once everyone finishes work.
      d. Running a non-credentialed scan first thing in the morning.

42. A security analyst monitoring the domain controller identifies the following attack:

```
Pinging 192.168.5.253 with 24456 bytes of data
Reply from 192.168.5.253 bytes 24456 time<1ms TTL=128
Reply from 192.168.5.253 bytes 24456 time<1ms TTL=128
Reply from 192.168.5.253 bytes 24456 time<1ms TTL=128
Reply from 192.168.5.253 bytes 24456 time<1ms TTL=128
```

Which of the following attacks is occurring?

      a. Ping of death.
      b. DNS poisoning.
      c. Buffer overflow.
      d. SQL injection.
      e. Remote-access trojan.
      f. Integer overflow.

43. Which of the following are considered among the best indicators that a received message is a hoax (choose TWO)?

      a. License violation.
      b. Warnings of monetary loss.
      c. Claims of possible damage to the computer.
      d. Event logs filling up.
      e. Certificate trust error.

44. A threat actor purchases an exploit from the dark web to launch an attack. Name the threat actor.

       a. Organized crime.
       b. Malicious insider.
       c. Script kiddie.
       d. Competitor.
       e. Hacktivist.

45. What type of threat actor would attend a political rally?

       a. Organized crime.
       b. Malicious insider.
       c. Script kiddie.
       d. Competitor.
       e. Hacktivist.

46. A security administrator has completed a monthly review of DNS server query logs. He notices persistent TCP connections to a remote server carrying megabytes of data each day. Which of the following is the most likely explanation for this anomaly?

       a. An attacker is stealing large amounts of proprietary company data.
       b. Employees are playing multiplayer computer games.
       c. A worm is attempting to spread to other hosts via SMB exploits.
       d. Internal hosts have become members of a botnet.

47. Which of the following can be implemented to prevent a local LAN attack?

       a. `arp -s`.
       b. `dig -n`.
       c. `arp -a`.
       d. `netstat -an`.
       e. `tcpdump -`.

48. A black box penetration tester has managed to access the following registry key: `HKEY_LOCAL_MACHINE\Software\Microsoft\Windows\CurrentVersion\Run` What type of penetration-testing technique did he use?

       a. Privilege escalation.
       b. Pivoting.
       c. Regression testing.
       d. Active reconnaissance.

49. The CISO has written a policy informing the IT team that he wants company personnel to be able to make changes to data and delete documents. Which of the following titles should he use for the policy?

> a. On-boarding policy.
> b. Acceptable-use policy (AUP).
> c. Least-privilege policy.
> d. Separation-of-duties policy.

50. The company is upgrading the computers for the customer services department, and the cybersecurity team have built an image to roll out. Which of the following is the best security reason that an image was used for the deployment?

> a. To enable the computers to boot securely.
> b. To ensure that the same applications are deployed.
> c. To reduce the number of updates.
> d. To ensure that the computers have the same baseline.

Cheat Sheet

The cheat sheet is a condensed format of the main facts that you need to know before taking the exam. We must learn the exam concepts and not just the answers to a bank of questions.

Malware

- Virus – replicates using port `1900`
- Polymorphic virus – mutates, as does its hash value
- Ransomware – asks for money; could be subtle
- Worm – spreads using port `5000`
- Trojan – could change `.dll` files
- Rootkit – upon reinstalling the OS, it is still there; in Linux, look for the bash shell as a path
- Keylogger – logs keystrokes
- Adware – uses popups
- Bots – infected machine used as an attack vector
- RAT – sends back passwords to the hacker, who then logs in
- Logic bomb – needs a trigger, such as time

Attacks – Social Engineering

- Phishing – uses email; targets one person
- Spear phishing – attacks a group; look for plurals in the question
- Whaling – attacks CEO or high-level executives
- Vishing – uses a telephone or leaves a voicemail
- Tailgating – follows someone through; does not use credentials
- Impersonating – pretends to be from the help desk or IT team
- Dumpster diving – pulls information from the trash bin
- Shoulder surfing – someone looks over an employee's shoulder or uses a smartphone to video your bank transaction
- Watering hole – infects a trusted website
- Authority – email from CEO or HR; asks you to fill in a form
- Urgency – letting a fireman into the server room

Attacks – Application

- DoS – one host taking out another
- DDoS – multiple hosts taking out one host
- Man-in-the middle – interception attack data in real time
- Replay – interception attack data replayed at a later date
- Kerberos – prevents replay and pass-the-hash attacks
- Buffer overflow – too much data in a field
- Integer overflow – too large a number in a data field
- XSS – uses HTML tags/JavaScript; no authentication
- XSRF/CSRF – asks you to click on an icon and provide authentication
- Privilege escalation – tries to get admin rights
- ARP poisoning – prevented by using static entries in the arp cache—for example, `arp -s`
- ARP – local LAN attack
- DNS poisoning – prevented by using DNSSEC that produces RRSIG records
- Man-in-the-browser – trojan already installed; after bank transactions; URL does not change

- Zero-day virus – cannot be detected other than baseline; takes more time to get antidote
- Pass-the-hash – attacks NTLM authentication; prevented by disabling NTLM or using Kerberos
- Session hijacking – steals your cookies

Wireless Attacks

- Evil twin – looks like a legitimate WAP
- Rogue AP – free; steals information; prevented by using 802.1x
- Jamming – interference attack
- WPS – push the button; brute-force attacks underlying password
- Bluejacking – hijacks Bluetooth phone; sends text messages
- Bluesnarfing – steals contacts from Bluetooth phone
- RFID – prevents theft of small devices
- NFC – wireless payment; short range
- Disassociation attacks – prevents access to the WAP

Cryptographic Attacks

- Birthday – hash-collision attack; digital signatures vulnerable
- Rainbow tables – precomputed list of passwords and hashes; used for hash-collision attacks
- Dictionary – password; prevented by using a random character in your password or misspelling your password
- Brute force – every available combination; prevents account lockout low value or salt password
- Collison – matches hashes
- Downgrade – uses legacy SSL rather than TLS; POODLE is a classic example
- Weak implementation – uses WEP; better to use WPA2-CCMP as it is the strongest

Threat Actors

- Script kiddie – purchases scripts and programs, probably from the dark web
- Hacktivist – politically motivated agent
- Organized crime – profit-driven agent who will blackmail you
- Nation state/APT – foreign government agent
- Insider – known as a malicious insider; hardest to detect
- Competitors – steals your trade secrets; beats you to market with your product

Penetration Testing

- Intrusive – can cause damage
- Black box – knows nothing
- White box – knows everything
- Gray box – has at least one piece of information—for example, a password or diagram
- Fuzzing – enters random characters into an application for spurious results; black-/white-box pen testers use it
- Pivot – accesses a network through a vulnerable host, then attacks a secondary, more important host
- Initial exploitation – where pen testing starts
- Escalation of privileges – obtains admin rights
- Intrusive scan – used in pen testing; can cause damage to your system

Vulnerability Scanning

- Passive – no damage
- Credentialed – admin rights; more information; audit files; account and certificate information
- Non-credentialed – low level; finds missing patches
- Identify lack of security controls or misconfiguration

Vulnerability Impact

- Race condition – two threads accessing data at the same time
- End-of-life systems – lack of vendor support; no patches
- Error handling – customer side makes error small; IT support error needs all information
- Default configuration – changes username or passwords
- Resource exhaustion – running CPU at 100% or running out of memory
- Untrained users – not complying with policies
- Key management – ensures keys signed in and out each day

2
Technologies and Tools Practice Tests

A security professional must have knowledge of the different tools that they have at their disposal to identify threats and attacks on the network.

The first area that we will look at is installing and configuring network components such as different types of firewalls. We'll then look at how VPNs operate with their different components and operate with different scenarios. We will also look at NIPS, NIDS, HIPS and HIDS, proxy servers, load balancers, wireless access points, mail gateways, and SIEM systems. We will also look at using DLP to prevent sensitive information from leaving the network, and finally, using NAC to ensure that the devices used for remote connections to the network are fully patched.

Next, we will be using the appropriate tools to access the security posture of a system, including protocol analyzers, network scanners, wireless scanners, and password crackers. We will look at data sanitization tools such as shredding, pulverizing, pulping, and degaussing. Security teams need to know about honeypots to determine the attack methods being used so we can mitigate against them. As a security administrator, you need to be familiar with command-line tools, different backup utilities, and the different types of scans (ranging from vulnerability scans to the more intrusive scans that would cause damage to your systems).

We need to be able to analyze and interpret the output from security tools such as HIDS/HIPS.

A security administrator needs the ability to troubleshoot common security issues such as certificate issues, unauthorized software, and different types of threats, including social engineering. We also need to troubleshoot applications and know when to use whitelists and blacklists.

A security administrator needs to familiarize themselves with deploying mobile devices securely, including connection methods, mobile device management concepts, different deployment models, understanding rooting/jailbreaking, and sideloading of applications.

A good knowledge of implementing secure protocols such as S/MIME, PGP, SRTP, SFTP, and securing data in transit using TLS and SSL.

Practice Test 5 – Open Questions – Technologies and Tools

Start off by answering the questions that you have the knowledge base to answer, then on a separate list write down the questions that you do not know the answers to, because you need to revise those areas before testing:

1. The ACL for a firewall has an allow rule for HTTP, HTTPS, and LDAP. What will happen when a user tries to download a file from an external FTP server?

2. A network administrator is configuring a switch and is unsure whether to enable port security or 802.1x. What can you advise on both of these technologies?

3. A security administrator is enabling IPSec on the file server that hosts the financial server. They are then going to enable IPSec between the server and all of the desktops being the financial users. What mode of IPSec will be adopted?

4. What type of firewall is best suited to deal with an incoming SYN flood attack?

5. A security administrator is enabling an L2TP/IPSec on a virtual private network. What will be the role of a VPN concentrator?

6. Your company is experiencing a very high volume of web traffic coming to their internet web servers. What is the best way to ensure that the people coming to your website get the web pages in a timely manner?

7. Your company is experiencing a high volume of DDoS traffic heading for your company's network. What is the best way to deal with this traffic?

8. What is the purpose of DNS round-robin, and what are the pitfalls of using it?

9. How can I capture the commands going to a network-based gaming application?

10. Your company provides internet access to films. What type of port should we use to ensure that the films run smoothly?

11. What type of tool can we use to determine the patch level version of a web server? Name three tools that can be used for this technique.

12. The security administrator has noticed a rise in the number of unauthorized hosts appearing on your network. What two tools can be implemented so that they are notified when someone attaches a new host?

13. The security administrator has noticed that there has been an increase in the number of failed logins attempts on network-based computers. The account lockout policy allows three failed login attempts. What type of tool can they use for real-time monitoring of these events?

14. The CEO has written a new policy stating that all of the security logs on domain controllers are to be copied to a central location daily. These log files need to be secured to ensure that they have not been tampered with after collection. What action should the security administrator take to fulfill this policy?

15. When an attack on a host is made, a connection is established. Which two tools can capture the established connection so that the attacker can be identified?

16. What data format cannot be analyzed by any of the company's monitoring tools?

17. What are the three main components of a proxy server?

18. What is the purpose of a reverse proxy?

19. What technique does an iPhone use to send software updates to the phone?

20. What is the danger of someone taking an unauthorized smartphone into a research and development laboratory?

21. If I am using my personal phone as a BYOD device, what can be done to keep business data separate from my personal data?

22. What would be a safe, restricted, and contained environment that an IT team could provide to contractors to use?

23. What would I need to use in conjunction with a mobile device to limit the bandwidth being used when I download applications to the device?

24. If I want to use a third-party application on my carrier-locked iOS phone, what two stages should I perform to enable the application to run?

25. If I want to use a third-party application on my carrier-locked Android phone, what two stages should I perform to enable the application to run?

26. In what circumstances would I remote-wipe a device using the mobile device management system; (name two)?

27. The network administrator has been receiving support calls relating to the wireless access point. What tool should they use to diagnose the problem?

28. When the SSID of a wireless access point has been disabled, what two types of devices can be used to discover the SSID?

29. When I was on holiday in Las Vegas, all of the pictures I submitted to Facebook had the location where the picture was taken. Which tool carried out the labeling of photographs?

30. Which tools can I use to see if the DLL files of an application have been altered or tampered with?

31. When setting up certificates on a mobile device, the administrator is receiving certificate trust errors. What two actions should the administrator carry out first?

32. A new employee was given a company laptop with the correct certificates installed. Two weeks later, they report to the IT team that they are getting trust errors with the certificates. What has the new employee done to cause this error?

33. A salesperson cannot get internet access on their laptop, so they connect their 4G phone to the laptop to provide internet access. What technique have they just used?

34. A security administrator has found that many company devices have been tampered with over the past week. When they have looked into the security log files, they found that nothing out of the ordinary had been recorded. What has been tampering with the equipment?

35. A retailer wants to allow its customers to use a wireless payment method to pay for small transactions. What payment method must the customer adopt?

36. An audit has been carried out against the assets held by the IT team and the auditor has found that the company owns 300 Windows 10 licenses, but the software has been installed on 302 laptops. What is this violation known as?

37. A small company is going to purchase a firewall and needs to ensure that the firewall is an all-in-one device providing more protection than just simply being a firewall. What type of firewall would you recommend that they purchase?

38. A security administrator has found that remote users have been infecting the company network with viruses. What tool do they need to implement to mitigate this risk?

39. The security team has discovered that an attacker has been logging in twice to each machine but a security alert has not been logged as the company has an account lockout threshold of three attempts. What type of system should the company implement to alert them of any re-occurrence of this event?

40. What type of system does the security administrator need to implement to prevent anyone from emailing out credit card information?

41. What type of security technology can prevent a hacker from accessing a computer's registry remotely?

42. What common security issue reduces the amount of bandwidth available to the company coupled with reducing the amount of disk space available on a computer?

43. What security technology can be implemented on a virtual machine to protect it against attacks?

44. What security technology only allows approved applications to run on a system? How does it work?

45. Why would a security administrator archive security logs onto a WORM drive?

46. What type of security technology would an administrator implement to protect a web server's applications and data?

47. What is the purpose of push notification services?

48. A security administrator wants to implement a Bluetooth type of technology that uses low power. What technology should he implement?

49. A company has suffered from an increase in the theft of its high-end laptops. What technology can be implemented to prevent such laptops from being stolen?

50. A security administrator has discovered that the incorrect authentication information has been used to access the network. What type of technology is the attacker using?

Practice Test 6 – Fill The Gaps – Technologies and Tools

Fill-the-gaps questions really test your knowledge, and can be quite vague at times. In the CompTIA Security+ examination, some of the test questions can also be quite vague, hence the value of this section.

Complete the answers that you can, then make a list of those topics that you are getting wrong, as you need to revise these areas before you take the test. Best of luck.

In the following questions, fill in the gaps to make the statement. Each underlined section of the sentence represents one word—for example, _____ means that one word is missing; _____ _____ means that two words are missing:

1. Both the _____ and _____ use ACLs to block traffic by port, protocol, or IP address.

2. Where the router or firewall has no allow rule for a particular type of traffic, the traffic is blocked by a technique called _____ ____.

3. When setting up IPSec across the internet, it is used in _____ mode but when it is used in the LAN between client and server or server to server, it is known as _____ mode.

4. I have installed a _____ _____ is my DMZ so that it will decrypt incoming traffic so that my firewall or inline NIPS can _____ the traffic.

5. If I disable the SSID on my wireless access point, it can be discovered by a _____ _____ _____ as the SSID is included in the packet or an SSID _____ device.

6. The role of the VPN concentrator is to set up the _____ _____ before the exchange of data.

7. _____ _____ is used to prevent someone plugging a laptop into my network; however, _____ is used to prevent a rogue access point being plugged into my network as it authenticates the user or device itself.

8. A _____ is a device that is used by cybersecurity administrators so that they can observe the attack method used by hackers. This will then enable them to prevent these types of attacks in the future.

9. A security administrator has noticed in the SIEM system log files that an attack was detected on Server 1 but when they manually inspected the server, the attack was not shown; this is known as a _____ _____.

10. One of the reasons why a SIEM system records a false positive is because the wrong _____ _____ were being used, therefore it was monitoring the wrong type of attack.

11. An _____ NIPS has traffic flowing through it; however, the NIDS is known as _____ and relies on sensors and collectors to discover new attacks.

12. _____ _____ inspects traffic going to a website, whereas a _____ _____ inspects traffic across the network.

13. Banner grabbing uses tools such as Dimitri, _____, _____, and _____.

14. _____ shows established connections in a Windows environment, whereas _____ shows established connections in a Linux/Unix environment.

15. A _____ system correlates security logs from various devices such as servers and firewalls. The security administrator has decided to store the logs into a _____ drive so that they can be read but not tampered with as they may be needed as evidence at a later date.

16. A company could use a ____-__-____ VPN instead of an expensive lease line or even more expensive dark fiber, but it must be set to _____ - ___ mode.

17. A _____ _____ could be used as a spam filter and a ____ solution to prevent PII and sensitive information from leaving the company.

18. Both ____ and a _____ can detect when new hosts have been added to your internal network.

19. A _____-_____ NIDS/NIPS uses a known database and is reliant on regular updates where _____-_____ NIDS/NIPS start with a known database but can identify new variants.

20. A security administrator changes the default _____ and _____, disables the SSID, and enables _____ filtering to make a wireless access point more secure.

21. A security administrator sets up a wireless access point by inserting a password that will be used by ____. The user can now access the WAP by simply pushing a button; however, this could be subject to a _____-_____ password attack.

22. An auditor reports to a security administrator that the company's wireless network could be detected on the footpath outside of the premises. The security administrator then uses ___ _____ _____ antenna to mitigate the risk of being attacked by an external threat actor.

23. A new company has an increasing amount of people coming to its website; therefore, it can use a _____ _____ or ___ _____ _____ to ensure that incoming web requests were dealt in a timely manner.

24. A company installed a _____ firewall to deal with DDoS traffic trying to attack their company's website.

25. A company has set up account lockout with three attempts. An attacker tries to log in once to three separate hosts but finds himself locked out. This is because a _____ system has a _____ engine.

26. If a company was to use weak passwords, they would set them with a low minimum _____ _____ to mitigate the risk of being attacked or could use a _____ _____ ____-_____ _____ as a compensating control.

27. There have been attacks on the company's virtual machine network, therefore, the security administrator has installed a _____ on each machine to protect them.

28. A company has set a policy of using **mobile device management** (**MDM**) to _____ _____ lost or stolen machine to mitigate the risk of data falling into the wrong hands.

29. _____ can be used to stop PII and sensitive information from leaving the company via email or being exported onto a USB drive.

30. The security team in a company are now using _____ to ensure that company laptops can remain within the company's premises. Another method would be RFID.

31. One of the company's employees uses _____/_____ so that they can unlock a mobile phone. They now want to install a third-party application. This is known as _____.

32. _____ is a secure protocol that can be used to run remote commands securely on routers or directory services. It can also use a graphical user interface.

33. If an application cannot run on a desktop, it could well be that the application is just not on the _____. It does not necessarily need to be on the blacklist. It may not be on any list.

34. If I want to restrict a user's ability to log in to ensure that they can only authenticate when they are in the United States of America and ensure that they cannot authenticate from any other location. This form of authentication is known as _____-_____ _____.

35. _____ is first and foremost a firewall, but it can also carry out the functions of URL and content inspection and _____ _____.

36. An organization was suffering from DNS poisoning and decided to use _____ to encrypt the DNS traffic with TLS. This produced both DNSKEY and _____ records.

37. When two people wish to send digitally signed and encrypted emails, they could use _____ for email integrity and PGP for _____.

38. When people decide to leave the company for a highly paid job, we should carry out ___ _____ to ensure that the company CYOD equipment has been returned, followed by an _____ _____ by the human resources department.

39. A company has decided that instead of the sales staff traveling to the head office for weekly meetings, they will use videoconferencing. The videoconferencing should be secure, therefore they will use the _____ protocol.

40. The company has decided to keep the employees' personal data separate from the business data by using either _____ or storage _____.

41. When the bandwidth coming into your company is being reduced and the space on one of your company servers is being aggressively reduced, this is a sign of downloading _____ _____.

42. You are a directory services administrator and use LDAP to create, search for, and find objects. The CISO has now written a policy requiring you to secure your session with the directory services. Therefore, you will use the _____ protocol and TCP port ____.

43. Security administrators can use _____ _____ to prevent anyone using a CD ROM or any other form of removable media to mitigate the risk of spreading a virus or stealing data.

44. Recently, data has been compromised from a mobile phone, and the CEO has asked the security team to come up with a solution to protect data at rest. The security team are going to use _____ _____ _____ to protect the data at rest and _____ _____ to prevent access to the mobile phones.

45. There have been certificate trust errors for the company website. The security team is going to check that the certificate is _____ and has been added to the _____ _____ certification authorities store on the web server.

46. Over the past year, a hospital has lost about 25 laptops from the consultant's offices when they were visiting the patients during ward rounds. The security team has now rolled out _____ to prevent the theft of these laptops.

47. A network team has rolled out _____ _____ to prevent unauthorized rogue DHCP servers from operating on the company network.

48. The CEO of a publishing company has told the IT team that they can no longer use FTP to download books as they need to adopt a protocol that can download large books securely. The chosen protocol was _____ as it is encrypted and uses two ports to download data.

49. A company has recently started using _____ to check the health of the remote user's laptop to ensure that they cannot spread a virus to the company's network.

50. The best method for sanitizing a hard drive is by _____ it. However, the best way of disposing of paper documents containing PII information is to _____ them.

Practice Test 7 – Drag and Drops – Technologies and Tools

I suggest using two different-colored pens: blue or black or answers that are easy for you to identify and a red or different-colored pen for answers that you are unsure of. This way, you can identify your strong and weak areas.

Place the answers into the relevant answer boxes in the following table, starting with the answers that you can easily identify. Make a list of those that you cannot answer on your first time through, as you need to revise those areas. Then use logic to answer the remaining questions.

Insert the phrases at the end of this section into the appropriate answer boxes in the following table. Each phrase can only be used once:

Description	Answers
Other than a firewall, what other device uses ACL?	
Setting up a non-secure remote session to your LAN.	
IPSec mode between two servers on your LAN.	
Add an application, EXE, or a DLL so it will run.	
The system does not detect an attack.	
What will you do if a mobile phone is lost or stolen?	
Prevent DNS poisoning by using DNSSEC. What records are created?	
On a firewall, the result when the traffic is not on the allow rules.	
Lets you monitor the attack methods used.	
Used to protect PII and sensitive information from leaving the company by email or USB.	
A NIPS where all the traffic flows through it.	
How to keep personal and business data separate on a cell phone.	
A tool that tells you the patch version of a web server.	
A firewall that can also perform malware inspection.	

IPSec mode in a site-to-site VPN.	
A passive device that works with a NIPS.	
A stolen Bluetooth phone used for texting your friends and family.	
A tool that can be used for banner grabbing.	
Can be used instead of a motion sensor to detect motion.	
Adding a third-party application to your phone.	
How to protect a mobile telephone.	
The system detects a virus but manual inspection contradicts it.	
Secure remote access protocol that can use a GUI to access a router.	
How you could block unwanted applications.	
Used for secure transfer of data between two hosts.	

Use the following options to answer the preceding questions:

Camera	Blacklist	TLS	False negative	Sideloading
DLP	Router	Remote wipe	SSH	Netcat
False positive	Implicit deny	Policy violation	Inline	Bluejacking
Tunnel mode	Banner grabbing	Honeypot	FDE, screen locks	Storage segmentation
NIDS	Transport mode	UTM	Whitelist	RRSIG

Practice Test 8 – Mock Exam 2

Start off the mock exam with a clean sheet of paper and note down the questions that you cannot answer or are guessing at, because you need to revise those areas. When you take this test, follow these instructions:

DO:

- Read the questions carefully. Do not scan. Draw diagrams on questions you are unsure of.
- Rule out the wrong answers to leave the correct answer.
- When you get the answers down to two answers there is a 50-50 chance of being right. Read the question again and look for the finer detail that will make one of those selections a 60-40.

- Flag up for review (top-right of screen) the questions that you don't like. Do not answer them as the review screen shows those items in red. Don't waste time trying to work them out at this stage.
- Before ending your review, go down the columns left to right and ensure all questions have an answer.
- End review—check all questions and answers and then end the exam.

DON'T:

- Scan the questions, especially if English is not your first language
- Second guess yourself
- Change answers
- Re-read the whole exam if you have spare time

Answer the following questions:

1. The network administrator has received a support call from the CEO stating that he cannot download a book from the internet. The publisher is using an FTP server for the book download. The firewall rules are shown as follows:

- Inbound rules
- HTTP port 80 allow
- HTTPS port 443 allow
- DNS port 53 allow

Which of the following options prevents the download? Choose the BEST answer.

    a. There is no allow rule for FTP traffic.
    b. There is an explicit deny rule.
    c. Implicit deny is preventing the download.
    d. He needs to change the web browser to support FTP traffic.

2. The network security team have been informed by the customer services department that visitors in the waiting area keep plugging their laptops into a spare wall jack to obtain internet access. The network team realize that this is a security risk. What is the BEST solution to prevent this?

    a. Ask customers to hand their laptops into reception when they arrive.
    b. Enable 802.1x on the router to prevent internet access.
    c. Place a sign in the waiting room.
    d. Enable port security on the router to prevent internet access.
    e. Enable port security on the switch.

3. A network administrator has just informed the cyber security team that he is going to set up network access control using host health checks without using a quarantined network. Which of the following best describes what will happen if a host is non-compliant?

    a. The remote client will not be authenticated.
    b. The remote client will be authenticated then the connection will drop.
    c. The remote client will be authenticated.
    d. The remote client will not be authenticated and the connection will be successful.

4. The network team have just installed another switch into the network and the network traffic is going extremely slowly. What can they do to ensure the traffic has less latency?

    a. Use a packet sniffer to identify which traffic is going slowly and deny it access to the network.
    b. Use spanning tree protocol to prevent looping.
    c. Reduce the number of VLANs on the switch.
    d. Use a network load balancer to balance the traffic.

5. The systems administrator went to a local shop for lunch and paid using a contactless payment method. Which of the following connection methods was he using to purchase lunch?

    a. Wi-Fi
    b. Cellular
    c. NFC
    d. KFC
    e. Bluetooth

6. A network administrator is setting up a new VPN server and is using a CISCO VPN Series 3000 concentrator. What is the purpose of the VPN concentrator?

    a. It increases the concurrent connections on the VPN.
    b. It allows the VPN to connect to a RADIUS server.
    c. It allows the VPN to connect to a TACACS+ server.
    d. It establishes the secure sessions for the VPN.

7. Your company network has recently been attacked by remote users. The cyber security team need to use tools that will identify the established sessions so that they can be identified. Which of the following tools will show established sessions? Choose two.

    a. Protocol analyzer
    b. Netstat

       c. Netcat (nc)
       d. Tcpdump

8. During an internal audit, users complained that the quality of the videoconferencing has been intermittent. What is the BEST solution to ensure a better videoconferencing experience?

       a. Ensure that they are using SRTP instead of RTP.
       b. Use a VPN.
       c. Put the voice traffic into a VLAN.
       d. Use an iSCSi connector.

9. An exchange engineer has recommended that the mail server is upgraded as the current mail protocol does not keep a copy on the server. What mail protocol is being used?

       a. POP 3
       b. HTTPS
       c. TLS
       d. IMAP4
       e. Webmail

10. The auditor has carried out an inspection of the finance department and has made recommendations, that the file server holding the financial data and the desktops of the financial department should use IPSec to secure the sessions between them. The network administrator has asked the security analyst what mode of IPSec should be used? What did the security analyst recommend?

       a. IPSec in tunnel mode
       b. IPSec in split tunnel mode
       c. IPSec in transport mode
       d. IPSec in full tunnel mode

11. What are the similarities and differences between a proxy server and a UTM firewall? Choose all that apply.

       a. The proxy server can perform malware inspection.
       b. The UTM can perform malware inspection.
       c. The proxy server can perform URL filtering.
       d. The UTM can perform URL filtering.
       e. The proxy server can perform content filtering.
       f. The UTM can perform content filtering.
       g. The proxy server can perform web page caching.
       h. The UTM can perform web page caching.

12. The system administrator has just installed a new finance application onto the financial director's laptop. The application will not run and the event viewer shows an error running the `payroll.dll`. What is the BEST solution to ensure that the application works?

    a. Add the application to the whitelist.
    b. Add the application to the blacklist.
    c. Add the application's EXE file to the whitelist.
    d. Add the DLL binary for the payroll application to the whitelist.
    e. Remove the DLL binary for the payroll application from the blacklist.

13. A security administrator installed a new inline NIPS that has been inspecting all traffic flowing through it with great success. A medium sized packet flowing through the inline NIPS could not be inspected. What is the BEST reason that it could not be inspected?

    a. The packet was not recognized by the NIPS
    b. The packet was encrypted before arriving at the NIPS
    c. The NIPS was using the wrong input filter
    d. The NIPS had an exception rule for the packet

14. A cyber security team has carried out an audit of the mail server and has recommended that mail between the mail servers must not be monitored or captured by protocol analyzers. The mail must remain confidential. Which of the following protocols should the auditor recommend?

    a. POP secure
    b. IMAP secure
    c. TLS
    d. SSL
    e. HTTPS

15. A company refurbishes a lecture theatre with state-of-the-art presentation equipment valued at over $25,000. What can the security administrator install to prevent the theft of the equipment from the theatre? Choose the BEST answer.

    a. NFC
    b. Geolocation
    c. Asset tracking
    d. Tagging

16. Which of the following authentication systems could allow a user access to a system while creating an access violation?

    a. Smart card authentication
    b. Username and password authentication

        c. Biometric authentication
        d. Federation services authenticated

17. The financial director stores credit card information on his laptop. Therefore, the cyber security team have installed full disk encryption to prevent exfiltration of this data. A DLP solution has also been installed to prevent PII and sensitive information such as credit cards from leaving the laptop via USB drive or email. What can be installed on his laptop to prevent remote attacks?

        a. HIDS
        b. HIPS
        c. NIDS
        d. NIPS

18. A company is removing its expensive lease line between London and Glasgow sites and is going to replace it with a VPN solution. What type of VPN will they use as a replacement and which mode is the BEST to use? Choose two.

        a. L2TP/IPSec
        b. IPSec transport mode
        c. Always on mode
        d. IPSec tunnel mode
        e. Site-to-site VPN
        f. PPTP VPN
        g. SSL VPN

19. A network administrator needs to be alerted when new hosts join the network. Which of the following tools can help them to achieve this? Choose two.

        a. HIDS
        b. Nmap
        c. Netstat
        d. NIDS

20. The security administrator needs to purchase a new biometrics authentication system for a multinational corporation. Which of the following products will he decide is the BEST option to purchase?

        a. Product A – low FAR
        b. Product B – high FAR
        c. Product C – high FRR

d. Product D – low FRR
e. Product E – low CER
f. Product F – high CER

21. The cyber security team have been collecting the security logs from all of the servers and network appliances and storing them in a WORM drive. Why have they chosen this type of drive? Select the MOST suitable answer.

a. It can be protected by a password.
b. It is a portable drive that can be locked away at night.
c. It is an industry-standard drive for cyber security.
d. The information cannot be altered.

22. A systems administrator for a large multinational company is replacing 1,000 hard drives from company desktops. Which of the following data sanitation tools should he use to destroy the data on the old hard drives?

a. Pulverizing
b. Degaussing
c. Low-level formatting
d. Shredding

23. A cyber security analyst obtained the following information:

John Scott   5f4dcc3b5aa765d61d8327deb882cf99

Which tool did the cyber security analyst use and what does it represent? Choose two.

a. It is his employee ID.
b. Packet sniffer.
c. Password hash.
d. Hash of his employee ID.
e. Password cracker.
f. Wireless scanner.

24. The backup operator backs up the company data on a daily basis. Which of the following is the fastest backup?

a. Full backup
b. Differential backup
c. Snapshot
d. Incremental backup

25. A SIEM system notifies the system administrator that a computer with a hardened operating system has a vulnerability. When a manual check is done, no vulnerabilities exist. Why is the system producing the wrong information? Choose the BEST two options.

    a. The SIEM system is missing some system updates.
    b. The SIEM system is using the incorrect input filters.
    c. The host-based firewall is preventing monitoring.
    d. The SIEM system is producing false negatives.
    e. The SIEM system is producing false positives.

26. The cyber security team wish to prevent mobile devices from operating outside of the United Kingdom. What is the best way to achieve this?

    a. Geolocation
    b. GPS tracking
    c. Context-aware authentication
    d. All of the above

27. Your company has been very successful and has an enormous volume of web traffic coming to the company's web servers. However, the load balancer has failed and you are waiting for a replacement. What can we use to manage the web traffic coming in until a new load balancer arrives?

    a. NAT server
    b. Stateful firewall
    c. Round robin
    d. Stateless firewall

28. You are a systems administrator for a company hosting the G4 summit. Which of the following data sanitation tools should you use to destroy all of the paperwork used in the summit?

    a. Shred
    b. Burn
    c. Pulverize
    d. Pulp

29. An auditor from FAST carried out an audit of the company software and made three observations:

Product	Licenses	In use
A	100	102
B	25	26
C	30	41

Which of the following BEST describes the auditor's recommendations?

    a. Company policy violation
    b. Overuse of licenses
    c. License compliance violation
    d. License compliance warning

30. There has been a number of successful cyber attacks on corporate websites where hackers have managed to steal credit card information. What is the BEST way for your cyber security team to discover the attack methods used?

    a. Speak to a company that was attacked
    b. Read bulletins from security websites
    c. Set up a honeynet
    d. Monitor the SQL database holding the information

31. An auditor was carrying out a network audit on the wireless network that was not broadcasting the SSID. He managed to use two different tools to discover the SSID. Which two tools did he use?

    a. Tcpdump
    b. SSID decloak device
    c. Wireless scanner
    d. Protocol analyzer
    e. Packet sniffer

32. The backup operator backs up the company data on a daily basis. Which of the following is the fastest physical backup?

    a. Full backup
    b. Differential backup
    c. Snapshot
    d. Incremental backup

33. The network team have placed the voice traffic in a VLAN so that it is segmented from the rest of the network and has guaranteed bandwidth. The auditor has recommended that the voice traffic should be secured so that it cannot be monitored or captured by a protocol analyzer. Which of the following protocols should the network team select?

      a. SCP
      b. SFTP
      c. SRTP
      d. TLS

34. The cyber security team is rolling out new mobile phones that will hold sensitive company data. Which of the following is the BEST solution to protect the phones? Choose three.

      a. Context-aware authentication
      b. Strong password
      c. Device encryption
      d. TLS encryption
      e. GPS tracking
      f. Cable locks
      g. Screen locks

35. Which of the following protocols should secure traffic in transit between two mail servers?

      a. SSL
      b. HTTPS
      c. S/MIME
      d. TLS

36. A sales person logged into the company VPN to download some files. During the download, the sales person went online to look at the availability for flights for next month. During this session, the company network was hacked by someone gaining access via the web browser. What was the vulnerability that caused the attack?

      a. Man-in-the-browser attack
      b. Man-in-the-middle attack
      c. Split tunneling
      d. Session hijacking

37. A member of the sales team managed to connect remotely to the company network, but then a few seconds later his laptop was placed in a quarantine network and was asked to contact the remediation server. Why was this done?

    a. The remediation server must scan all incoming traffic to prevent a virus attack.
    b. The sales person's password has just expired.
    c. Network access control disabled the salesperson's account.
    d. The device that the salesperson's logged in with was not fully patched.

38. A small company has only one wireless access point, but today nobody can connect to the network. What tool should the system administrator use to troubleshoot, and why is the wireless access point not working?

    a. Protocol analyzer
    b. Tcpdump
    c. SSID decloak device
    d. Wireless scanner

39. A company has over twelve wireless access points that need to be configured centrally. How will this be achieved with the minimum amount of effort?

    a. Set up and roll out a group policy.
    b. Use a fat wireless controller.
    c. Update the wireless controllers using SSH.
    d. Use a thin wireless controller.
    e. Update the wireless access points using SNMP v 3.

40. A network administrator has just installed a new firewall and finds that traffic cannot flow through it. What is the default setting for a firewall? Choose the BEST two answers.

    a. Allow only HTTP and HTTPS traffic.
    b. Block all traffic.
    c. Allow by exception.
    d. The firewall is switched off and needs to be powered on.

41. A cyber security analyst needs to run a scan to discover the hostname, IP address, and missing patches on three separate servers without causing any damage to them. What is the BEST type of scan for him to use?

    a. Intrusive scan
    b. Non-credentialed scan
    c. Credentialed scan
    d. Active scan

42. The financial director has notified the IT director that employees have been emailing VISA credit card details to outside agencies. One of the programmers inserted a regular expression into an XML template, so that if any emails matches the following pattern, that mail will automatically get blocked:

```
^(?:4 [0-9] {12] (?: {0-9] {3} )?
```

What type of technology is being adopted to prevent the credit card details being emailed out?

       a. DLR
       b. NFX
       c. NFC
       d. DLP

43. What do a SIEM server and Kerberos have in common? Choose the BEST answer.

       a. They work in real time.
       b. You need admin rights to access them.
       c. They require time synchronization with the atomic clock.
       d. They are both Microsoft products.

44. The network administrator needs to ensure that the data passing through the inline NIPS is decrypted. Which of the following devices will he use to decrypt incoming packets?

       a. Load balancer
       b. Stateful firewall
       c. Proxy server
       d. Reverse proxy
       e. UTM
       f. WAF

45. A salesperson arrives at his hotel at 6:30 pm and realizes that he should have made a credit card payment today. He checks into his room and finds that the free Wi-Fi does not have any encryption. What is the BEST solution that he should take to ensure the payment is as secure as possible? Choose two, each providing part of the solution.

       a. Connect to the hotel Wi-Fi.
       b. Use a L2TP/IPSec VPN to connect to the credit card portal.
       c. Tether his phone to his laptop.
       d. Use SSL encryption to connect to the credit card portal.
       e. Use a SSL VPN to connect to the credit card portal.

46. Your company has been very successful and has an enormous volume of web traffic coming to the company's web servers. What can you use to help manage the web requests in a timely fashion?

    a. NAT server
    b. Stateful firewall
    c. UTM
    d. Load balancer

47. What is the most common method of authentication? Choose two.

    a. PIN
    b. Password
    c. CAC card
    d. Username
    e. Smart card
    f. Biometrics

48. A person at a market stall advertises that he can unlock a mobile and add third-party applications to your phone without the vendor finding out. Which of the following options is he using to achieve this? Choose two.

    a. Screen locks
    b. Routing/jailbreaking
    c. Degaussing
    d. Third-party app store
    e. Sideloading

49. Your company has been very successful and has an enormous volume of DDoS traffic coming to the company's web servers. What can you use to deal with the DDoS traffic? Choose the best answer.

    a. NAT server
    b. Stateful firewall
    c. Load balancer
    d. UTM

50. A network technician is going to set up a L2TP/IPSec VPN so that salespeople can remotely connect to the company offices. He needs to set up the VPN with the most secure protocol and the appropriate mode for its purpose. Which mode and encryption level with be used? Choose two.

        a. IPS transport mode
        b. Always on mode
        c. IPSec tunnel mode
        d. 3DES
        e. AES
        f. RS

Cheat Sheet

The cheat sheet is a condensed format of the main facts that you need to know before taking the exam. We must learn the exam concepts and not just the answers to a bank of questions.

Access Control Lists (ACLs)

- Firewalls and routers use ACL. No allow rule means implicit deny.

Firewalls

- Unified Threat Management (UTM)– all in one URL and content filter
- Stateful firewall – inspect deep into the packet, including size and commands
- Stateful firewall – protects against DDoS attacks
- Web application firewall – protect the web server and web applications
- Host-based – only protects the local computer
- Network-based – only protects the network

Network Protection

- **Network Intrusion Prevention System** (**NIPS**) – additional layer of protection placed close to firewall
- **Network Intrusion Detection System** (**NIDS**) – detects changes in network, uses sensor and collectors, and alerts the NIPS
- Signature-based – work from a local database
- Anomaly-based – start with a database but can learn new patterns

Proxy Server

- URL filter
- Content filter
- Caches web pages

Reverse Proxy

- Authenticates incoming connections
- Decrypts incoming traffic

Load Balancer

- Deals with a high load of web traffic
- Sends traffic to the least utilized host
- Affinity – sends the host to the same web server
- Round robin – balances traffic using DNS A records

SIEM System

- Real-time monitoring
- Correlates events on the network
- Measures account lockout, even with attempts on different computers
- Needs the correct filter, otherwise false position

Tools

- Packet sniffer/protocol analyzer – analyze network traffic
- Banner grabbing – analyze web server
- Banner grabbing – three main tools: Telnet, Nmap, and Netcat (nc)
- Nmap – maps out whole network – identifies new hosts
- NAC – ensures network clients are fully patched
- DLP – prevents exfiltration of PII, sensitive information, or credit card details
- Mail gateway – filters out spam
- Wireless scanner – troubleshoots WAP problems
- Wireless scanner and SSID decloak device – finds the SSID even if it's disabled
- Password cracker – can find the hash of a password
- Honeypot – looks like a legitimate website with lower security
- Honeypot – analyzes attack methods being used

Data Sanitization Tools

- Hard drive – best to worst: shred, pulverize, then degauss
- Paper – best to worst: pulping then shredding
- Paper – classified – burn bag – destroy by third party – certificate given

Command-Line Tools

- Netstat – shows established connection
- Netcat (nc) – shows established connections on Linux
- Tcpdump – Linux packet analyzer
- Nslookup – troubleshoot DNS issues
- DIG – Linux – troubleshoot DNS issues

Mobile Devices

- Mobile device management – policies and management of mobile devices
- Download manager – controls download speed
- Remote wipe – lost or stolen devices – back to factory reset
- Camera – can record videoconferencing, conversations, or take pictures
- Protect access – screen locks and strong passwords
- Protect data at rest – FDE – Full Disk Encryption or small devices Full Device Encryption
- Containerization/storage segmentation – separates private and business data
- BYOD – needs AUP and on/offboarding policies
- Geofencing – prevent theft of devices
- Geolocation – shows the location of the device
- Carrier unlocking – jailbreaking/rooting followed by sideloading the app

3
Architecture and Design Practice Tests

As a security professional, you must be aware of what is required when you're rolling out IT systems so that they are compliant with local laws. The first area we are going to look at is industry-standard frameworks and reference architectures. You need to understand that policies are derived from regulatory frameworks, but you must have knowledge of non-regulatory frameworks and national and international laws. Also, some insights into vendor and user guides and knowing how the defense in depth model operates is mandatory.

The second area that we must have knowledge of is how to implement a secure network, including intranets, extranets, DMZ, NAT, and the use of honeypots. Network segmentation needs to be designed and the correct placement of security devices such as firewalls, NIPS, and NIDS to ensure your networks are safe.

The next area where expertise is required is the rolling out of devices such as laptops and ensuring that they are hardened to protect the data residing on them. We will look at strong passwords, screen locks, and device encryption to protect data at rest. The security of embedded systems such as IoT items ranging from wearable technology, refrigerators, and home automation are vital as there is an ever-increasing use for these devices.

Companies will create many bespoke applications by using a secure software development life cycle from the development phase through testing and staging. They will use a white box pen tester that will evaluate the application before rolling them into production. Knowledge of secure coding techniques is required.

Two more areas that are evolving are virtualization and cloud services. Due to this, you must be aware of a virtual network's need for sandboxing, snapshots, and attacks on virtual machines, including VM escape. Security professionals need to know which cloud model is the most appropriate to use in different scenarios ranging from private, public and so on.

Last but not least, physical security controls such as cable locks, mantraps air gaps, biometric systems, security guards, and the use of cameras and CCTV will be tested in the Security+ exam.

Before you begin with each set of tests, you need to keep a sheet of paper handy so that the areas that you get wrong or are guessing the answers to have been written down so that you can identify the weak areas that you need to revise before the exam.

After the test, there is a *Cheat Sheet* section, which contains the most relevant information that you need in a short format. You must know all of the information in this section before you complete to take the exam.

Practice Test 9 – Open Questions – Architecture and Design

Start off by answering the questions that you have the knowledge base to answer, then on a separate list write down the questions that you do not know the answers to, because you need to revise those areas before testing:

1. What type of documents should I review prior to creating policy documents related to the company's computer systems?

2. What type of frameworks are COBIT and ITIL and are they legally enforceable?

3. Why would a multinational company purchase broadband from two different companies at the same time?

4. What is the name of the boundary layer between the LAN and WAN and what is the name of the web server located there?

5. What would be the reason for the IT team to air gap a laptop computer?

6. When a company sets up full device encryption on a laptop, what hardware must be built into the motherboard to store the keys?

7. Why would the IT security team roll out a honeypot and what would the benefits be?

8. You are the network administrator and need to deal with a high volume of website traffic, as well as an exceptionally large volume of DDoS traffic. What device(s) would you use?

9. A company has two different locations and has been paying $10,000 a year for a leased line. How can they connect the two locations with a much cheaper solution?

10. How can a security analyst capture the network traffic going to one port on the switch?

11. What is the role of a VPN concentrator?

12. What type of trust model is being used if I install BitLocker on my laptop to provide full disk encryption?

13. Why would a company make standard operating procedures?

14. The company research and development department needs a laptop for one of its employees. How should the security administrator set this machine up so that it isn't on the normal network but isolated?

15. Your company leases business units and you have four different companies located on the same switch. How should you set up the switch so that they remain isolated from the other companies?

16. The application whitelist is a list of approved applications and the blacklist is a list of banned applications. If my new application called `App1` does not run or install, is it because it is on the blacklist? What reason could there be for it not running or installing?

17. What common threat do printers and multi-functional devices both share as an attack vector against them?

18. A research and development department wants to test some applications that they have developed. However, some of these applications could be quite dangerous. What type of environment should the IT manager recommend for them to use but at the same time protect the company's existing network with?

19. Your company houses one of the largest data centers in Europe and they have just expanded a site in London. But since then, there have been fluctuations in temperature at only that site. What is causing this temperature change and how can this be remedied?

20. A professor has just automated most of his household gadgets using IoT technology. He told a colleague that it was very simple as all of the devices worked straight out of the box. What are two security measures that he may have overlooked?

21. What are the two categories of devices that refrigerators and defibrillators each come under?

22. How should a website developer set up the error information differently for the customer and the systems administrator?

23. What is fuzzing and what two entities would use it as part of their working practices?

24. What two secure coding techniques would a security administrator use to mask information and to embed information?

25. What is the best method to protect a SQL server against a SQL injection attack and what would a secondary method be?

26. What is the only technique that can be used to detect a zero-day attack?

27. What is one of the major benefits that a security administrator would gain by using an imaging package or machine template when rolling out new computers?

28. A security administrator has been told that one of his systems was categorized as an immutable system. Can you explain what method he will use for patch management?

29. A company wishes to move its bespoke applications to the cloud while still maintaining them. What model would they adopt?

30. How easy is it to customize a Software as a Service payroll package?

31. What are the main differences between Type I and Type II hypervisors?

32. If the US Army decided to move all of its systems to the cloud, what cloud model would they adopt?

33. What are the benefits that an IT training company receives by using cloud-based images for their classroom environments?

34. A newly formed company is going through a settling-in phase. They keep rewriting policy documents and none of the staff are sure what the latest policy on email is. What can the company do to alleviate their concerns?

35. When a new application is being tested with real data, what phase of the software development life cycle are they using?

36. Explain the main differences between waterfall and agile development life cycle models.

37. What type of physical security control would be used to capture moving images and at the same time provide non-repudiation?

38. What can be used within a company that uses a WLAN to prevent wireless communication from being captured by anyone outside of the company?

39. When you arrive at the company each morning, you must sign for your office key and when your working day ends, you must sign the key back in. What process is the company using?

40. What can a network administrator do with the cabling throughout the company to prevent rodents chewing through the cables and at the same time make it more secure?

41. If your company is adopting virtualization for its network, what danger does VM escape pose?

42. What danger does VM sprawl pose to your network security?

43. What security benefit does a NAT provide?

44. What can be used to prevent DNS poisoning and what resource records does it produce?

45. Why would a network administrator adopt DHCP snooping?

46. What is the security benefit of using COYD over BYOD?

47. What protocol does wireless credit card payment utilize?

48. If I am using my personal cell phone as a BYOD device, what can I use to keep my business data separate from that of my family and friends?

49. If my network load balancer is set to *affinity*, how does it differ from normal load balancing operations?

50. What can I use to manage a high volume of web traffic if my load balancer is broken?

Practice Test 10 – Fill The Gaps – Architecture and Design

Fill-the-gaps questions really test your knowledge base, and can be quite vague at times. In the CompTIA Security+ examination, some of the test questions can also be quite vague, hence the value of this section.

Complete the answers that you can, then make a list of those topics that you are getting wrong, as you need to revise these areas before you take the test. Best of luck.

In the following questions, fill in the gaps to make the statement. Each underlined section of the sentence represents one word—for example, _____ means that one word is missing; _____ _____ means that two words are missing:

1. Departmental isolation uses a _____, whereas a computer isolation uses _____.

2. A _____ is a boundary layer between the LAN and the _____. The website situated there is called an _____ and is normally accessed using a username and a password.

3. System _____ is where a virtual machine is running out of resources.

4. The best way to prevent a SQL injection attack is by using _____ _____. Another method is to use _____ validation.

5. A _____ is used is to hide the internal network, whereas _____ is multiple internal connections to one external connection.

6. _____ code is source code that is never used by the application.

7. A network intrusion detection system relies on _____ and _____ to sense changes to the local network.

8. An _____ switch can be used to connect multiple switches together and prevents looping.

9. The cloud model _____ as a Service is where you lease a bespoke application that cannot be _____ and is normally accessed via a web browser.

10. VM _____ is where an attacker gains access to a virtual machine and then attacks the host.

11. If a company has the account lockout set to a maximum of three attempts, an attacker can log in twice to all of the computer systems without being detected. However, if the company installs a _____ system that uses a _____ engine, once the third attempt is made, the attacker is locked out.

12. A company uses a lease line to connect two sites, London and Paris. Due to budget constraints, they are going to replace the lease line with a _____-__-_____ VPN using _____ __ mode.

13. When a SIEM system produces a _____ positive, it could be that the wrong _____ filter is being used.

14. _____ _____ is where companies in the same industry share the cost of creating and hosting a cloud-based application.

15. Group policy enforces policies for on-premise computers and _____
_____ _____ _____ enforces policies for cloud-based computers.

16. A waterworks and an oil _____ and both examples of _____ networks.

17. ___ _____ is where an unmanaged virtual machine has been placed on a virtual network. The administrator doesn't know about it, so it will not be patched and end up as a vulnerability on the network.

18. _____ can be used to mask data or code, whereas _____ is used to embed data inside other data.

19. _____ _____ is the cloud model that has more control, whereas _____ as a Service is the cloud service that has most control as you have to install, _____, and patch the operating system.

20. A company is building a new data center in Galway and is using _____ to control access to the data center and using a _____ system to help provide availability of the computer systems and prevent them from _____ and crashing.

21. A company has moved the desktops in the customer services departments so that people walking past the outside windows cannot _____ surf and has installed _____ _____ as an additional precaution.

22. _____ is the process of testing a new application with production _____. This can be carried out by using _____ to isolate them from the corporate network.

23. Using a master _____ to roll out desktop computers ensures that they have a consistent security _____.

24. Different occupations can be regulated by _____ _____ frameworks. An example of this would be PCI DSS for _____ _____ handling.

25. A high volume of web traffic can be controlled by using a _____ _____, whereas a high volume of DDoS traffic can be controlled by using a _____ _____ or a stateful _____.

26. A _____ box penetration tester can use a technique called _____ to carry out dynamic analysis of the _____ of a newly created application so that any _____ can be addressed.

27. PowerShell is an example of infrastructure as _____ where automation is paramount.

28. To protect data at rest on a laptop, full disk encryption can be used. However, this will require a _____ chip to be built into the laptop's motherboard.

29. The IT director is writing a new policy for the use of a new system and the technical lead is designing technical controls for this system. What they are both participating in is called _____ _____.

30. _____ _____ is derived from legislation and ensures compliance.

31. Using a mobile phone to provide internet access to a laptop is called _____.

32. The cybersecurity incident response team has launched a new _____ so that they can discover the new web-based attack methods being used.

33. A _____ __ _____ model is where the security team uses multiple layers of protection so that if one layer fails, the _____ layer should prevent the attack.

34. In a BYOD environment, inserting an SD card to keep business data separate from your personal data is an example of _____ _____, also known as _____.

35. ___-_____ configuration can be used to roll back to a previous state, should any unforeseen problems occur. In a virtual environment, a _____ can be used.

36. PGP uses a _____ __ _____, FDE uses a _____ _____ __ _____, and two separate _____ use a bridge of trust model, commonly known as a _____ _____.

37. A company has leased a SaaS application for its sales team, but they have complained about the interface and want customization to be carried out. The IT director has informed the sales team that these proposed changes _____ be made.

38. RAID 5 uses _____ parity and can lose _____ disk, whereas RAID 6 uses _____ parity and can afford to lose _____ disks. RAID __ is more resilient.

39. To secure a mobile phone, you should use _____ passwords, _____ _____, and full disk _____.

40. Vendor-specific _____ are rolled out with each piece of equipment to show you how they should be set up.

41. If a company wishes to move its bespoke applications to the cloud but still maintain them, it will adopt the cloud model _____ as a Service.

42. A refrigerator is an example of an _____ device, whereas a life support system is an example of _____.

43. _____ is a development life cycle model that requires the whole stage to complete before we move on to the next stage. _____ can start multiple stages at one time and its aim is customer satisfaction. It is similar to scrum.

44. The _____ _____ protocol is used for voice traffic over IP networks and the secure version is called _____.

45. _____ as a Service can provide identity management using _____ tokens.

46. Should a SIEM system find a false _____ on a known _____ operating system, it may be using _____ input filters.

47. Kerberos authentication and SIEM systems are both reliant on _____
_____.

48. To mitigate attacks on household IoT devices, ensure that the default _____ ____ _____ are changed _____ and that they cannot _____ access the internet.

49. A cybersecurity response team can capture all of the traffic going to one port on a switch using a _____ _____ or _____.

50. Containers are _____ virtual machines, whereas containerization is _____ _____ on a mobile device.

Practice Test 11 – Drag and Drop – Architecture and Design

I suggest using two different-colored pens: blue or black for answers that are easy for you to identify and a red or different-colored pen for answers that you are unsure of. This way, you can identify your strong and weak areas.

Place the answers into the relevant answer boxes in the following table, starting with the answers that you can easily identify. Make a list of those that you cannot answer on your first time through, as you need to revise those areas. Then use logic to answer the remaining questions.

Insert the phrases at the end of this section into the appropriate answer boxes in the following table. Each phrase can only be used once:

Description	Answer
A boundary layer between the LAN and the WAN.	
Taking a list of applications on a laptop two months apart.	
Prevents a SQL injection attack.	
A control that helps you rekey an ID badge.	
Testing an application with real data prior to going into production.	
Attack a virtual host from a guest virtual machine.	
Type of switch that connects multiple switches together.	
Used to isolate applications for patching, isolation, or testing.	
Wireless network for visitors or employees at lunchtime.	
The attack vector for visitors or employees.	
A life support machine is an example of this.	
Leasing a software package on the cloud.	
A control that mitigates risk.	
Putting an unmanaged VM onto a virtual network.	
To prevent an attack on a home IoT device, turn off the…	
Allows you to filter off traffic for analysis.	
A cloud model that gives you more control.	
A contained environment that's used to secure contractors' desktops.	
Isolation of a machine from the local network.	
Deploying your application into the cloud.	
Cloud model where companies share the cost of resources.	
A configuration that you can roll back.	
A cloud service that gives you more control.	
A web server located in the DMZ.	
Regulates temperature using hot and cold aisles.	

Use the following options to answer the preceding questions:

SoC	Internet connection	SaaS	IaaS	Extranet
HVAC	DMZ	Baseline	Staging	Stored procedure
VM sprawl	Technical	Tap or port mirror	Private cloud	Community cloud
VDI	Air gap	Administrative	PaaS	Non-persistent
VM escape	Aggregation	Sandboxing	Guest	Network interface

Practice Test 12 – Mock Exam 3

Start off the mock exam with a clean sheet of paper and note down the questions that you cannot answer or are guessing at, because you need to revise those areas. When you take this test, follow these instructions:

DOs:

- Read the questions carefully; do not scan. Draw diagrams on questions you are unsure of.
- Rule out the wrong answers to leave the correct answer.
- When you narrow the answers down to two possible answers, you have a 50–50 chance of being right. Read the question again and look for the finer details that will give one of those options a 60–40 chance of being right.
- Flag up for review (in the top-right of the screen) the questions that you don't like. Do not answer them, as the review screen will show those items in red. Don't waste time trying to work them out at this stage.
- Before ending your review, go down the columns from left to right and ensure that all questions have an answer.
- At the end, check all of the questions' answers and finish the exam.

DON'Ts:

- Scan through the questions, especially if English is your first language
- Second-guess yourself
- Change answers
- Reread the whole exam if you have spare time

Answer the following questions:

1. You are the systems administrator for a large multinational corporation that is going to open a new research and development department in their London office. The CEO has informed you that a new product is due to be released and he wants to prevent anyone logging into the research and development department's desktops. What is the BEST way for these laptops to be set up?

      a. VLAN
      b. Port forwarding
      c. Split tunnel
      d. Air gap

2. A company has rolled out new laptops with Windows 10; however, the auditor has observed that each of the laptops has different patches and updates. It has recommended that they are recalled and updated. Which of the following should have been done prior to the rollout to ensure they are patched?

      a. Application whitelist
      b. Secure baseline
      c. Blocklist
      d. Snapshot

3. The security administrator has received an updated security bulletin that mentions that some new attacks have appeared in the last week. The security industry does not have much information on the attack vectors. What action should they take to gather more information on the new attacks?

      a. Read the security bulletin weekly
      b. Roll out a honeypot
      c. Ensure Windows updates are current
      d. Ensure antivirus updates are current

4. A company is rolling out new mobile phones and needs to secure them from data theft. Which of the following items should be implemented? Choose three.

      a. Simple passwords
      b. Containerization
      c. Strong passwords
      d. Content manager
      e. FDE
      f. Antivirus
      g. Screen saver

5. Which of the following cloud models give you the MOST control?

   a. SaaS
   b. IaaS
   c. MaaS
   d. SECaaS
   e. PaaS

6. A sales person's company phone has broken and it will take two weeks to replace it so he has agreed to use his personal phone as a BYOD device. The security administrator is not happy that he will have personal and company data on the same device, so they will put a SD card into the phone to host the business data. What is this technique known as? Choose TWO.

   a. Separation
   b. Isolation
   c. Containerization
   d. Splitting
   e. Storage segmentation

7. What type of device category are tablets and life support systems? Select the BEST answer.

   a. Hybrid
   b. Digital
   c. SoC
   d. ICS
   e. Electronic

8. A multinational corporation is going to employee a group of 20 contractors for a six month period but want to create a secure environment for them to work in for that time. Which of the following would be the BEST solution?

   a. VDE
   b. VDI
   c. RDP
   d. SSH
   e. VPN

9. A systems administrator needs to choose a system that will provide fault tolerance and provides the most resilience. The system must be able to use four disks. Which of the following is the best choice?

> a. RAID 0
> b. RAID 1
> c. RAID 5
> d. RAID 6

10. A company is replacing its existing **Multi-Functional Devices** (**MFD**) with more modern versions. A risk assessment was carried out, listing potential attack vectors. Which of the following poses the GREATEST risk?

> a. Network interface
> b. Driver shimming
> c. Patching
> d. Default passwords
> e. Containerization
> f. Malicious insiders

11. An attacker managed to use an unmanaged virtual machine to attack the virtual machine host. The security administrator conducted lessons learned. During his report, why did he say the virtual machine was not hardened? Select the BEST choice.

> a. VM escape
> b. System sprawl
> c. Pivoting
> d. VM sprawl

12. Which of the following can prevent data emissions from leaving the company network?

> a. Security baseline
> b. Disconnect the network cable
> c. Patch management
> d. Faraday cage
> e. Host-based firewall

13. A developer, while creating a new application, has asked the cyber security analyst the best way for him to set up error handling. Which of the following options will the cyber security analyst recommend to the developer? Choose the three BEST answers.

> a. Users should see the full error as a long version with all the required details.
> b. The system administrator should see the full error as a long version with all the required details.

c. None of the errors should be logged so that the application runs.

d. All the errors should be logged and stop the application from running.

e. Users should see a shortened version of the error that is not detailed.

f. All the errors should be logged and the application should run.

g. The system administrator should see a shortened version of the error.

14. A company is looking for a software development life cycle model that is incremental and very similar to scrum. Which of the following is the BEST solution?

a. Agile

b. Waterfall

c. PRINCE 2

d. V-shaped model

15. Which of the following is a major benefit to a new successful company that's using cloud technologies? Select the BEST answer.

a. Redundancy

b. Cost

c. Elasticity

d. Security

16. Which of the following cloud models gives you more control?

a. Private

b. Public

c. Hybrid

d. Community

17. A company wants to ensure that their customers don't want to bring any lawsuits against them. Which of the following is the BEST to adopt?

a. Exceed regulatory framework standards

b. Exceed general-purpose guides

c. Exceed platform-specific guides

d. Exceed vendor-specific guides

18. A company needs to set up a web portal so that distributors can view their latest price list and order new products. Which of the following is the most suitable?

a. Intranet

b. LAN

    c. Extranet
    d. Internet
    e. DMZ

19. An attacker breaks into a company during the night and attempts to log into the employee's computers. The following is a log file from a real-time security system:

Computer 1 – login attempt 1
Computer 2 – login attempt 2
Computer 3 – login attempt 3 – locked out

What type of security system is this from?

    a. NIPS
    b. NIDS
    c. HIDS
    d. SIEM

20. A system administrator tried to install a bespoke piece of software but keeps getting errors. What action does the system administrator need to take? Choose the MOST likely answer.

    a. Remove the software from the blacklist
    b. Add the software to the blacklist
    c. Use a group policy to install the software
    d. Add the software to the whitelist
    e. Remove a group policy to prevent installation
    f. Remove the software from the whitelist

21. A network administrator is connecting more hosts to the network. Which of the following does he need install to help secure the network cables?

    a. Conduit
    b. Switch
    c. Router
    d. Flood guard

22. A systems administrator is upgrading a system when a problem occurs, resulting in the system crashing and being taken out of action. He was then able to roll back to the previous state. Which of the following was he using that allowed him to achieve this? Select the BEST answer.

    a. Imaging
    b. Baseline

c. Ghost

d. Non-persistent configuration

23. The cloud administrator needs to implement a cloud model when resources are shared. Which of the following should be implemented?

a. CASB

b. Private cloud

c. Public cloud

d. Community cloud

24. A multinational corporation suspects its **Chief Financial Officer** (**CFO**) of corruption and have contacted the cybersecurity administrator. The CEO has instructed him to capture all of the traffic flowing into the CFO's desktop. Which of the following is the MOST suitable?

a. Port mirror

b. Monitor the desktop with a SIEM

c. Mirror the disk activity

d. Use video capture software

25. The system administrator decided to put two legacy printers in their own VLAN while the modern printers were left on the network. Why did he choose to isolate the legacy printers? Select the BEST answer.

a. Legacy printers work better when placed in a VLAN

b. The legacy printers were contaminated with a virus

c. To enable them to print faster

d. There were no driver updates, making the printers vulnerable

26. What benefit does the security team get if all their computers had their operating system installed by using a master image? Select the BEST answer.

a. It saves time and resources

b. The computers are fully patched

c. It is very easy to implement

d. It provided a consistent security baseline

27. A security administrator has noticed that a dynamically expanding virus is attacking the company network. What is the first stage in protecting the network?

a. Reporting

b. Quarantine

c. Identifying the source
d. Recovery

28. A company has just built a new data center in Galway but they have noticed that 60% of the server's temperature has risen. What should they implemented to prevent this from happening? Select the BEST answer.

    a. More ventilation within the building
    b. Implement a mantrap
    c. Install ceiling fans
    d. Install a HVAC system
    e. Install a fire suppression system

29. A security administrator is rolling out new laptops to the sales team that will travel worldwide. What is the BEST method to secure the laptops?

    a. Least privilege
    b. Least functionality
    c. Fully patched
    d. Baseline
    e. Whitelist

30. A company wishes to move its customized applications to the cloud. Which cloud model should be selected?

    a. Software as a Service
    b. Infrastructure as a Service
    c. Monitoring as a Service
    d. Platform as a Service

31. A company has a virtual network suffering from an attack on one of its three host computers. After an investigation, it was established that the attacker gained access via a guest machine. What is this attack known as?

    a. Pivoting
    b. Remote exploit
    c. VM sprawl
    d. VM escape

32. The security administrators of a retail outlet have noticed that there has been a rise in the number of tablets being stolen from their sales staff. What should they implement to mitigate the risk of this happening in the future?

    a. Cable locks
    b. CCTV
    c. Change management
    d. Replace tablets with laptops

33. You are a cybersecurity administrator for a multinational airline that has an array of web servers that connect to a backend SQL database located in the DMZ. A hacker managed to carry out a SQL injection attack by using the phrase 1=1 in a SQL statement. What is the BEST way prevent future SQL injection attacks? Choose the BEST answer.

    a. Input validation
    b. Enable Kerberos
    c. SIEM system monitoring the SQL database
    d. Stored procedures

34. Which of the following cloud models is known as being multi-tenant?

    a. Public
    b. Private
    c. Hybrid
    d. Community

35. You are the systems administrator and have been testing a new application with production data. Which of the following describes what you are doing?

    a. Development
    b. Testing
    c. Staging
    d. Production
    e. White box testing

36. A security administrator has found out that an attacker has managed to insert more data than expected into a web-based application. He sets up input validation to prevent this type of attack. What type of attack had been carried out? Select the BEST answer.

    a. SQL injection
    b. Integer overflow
    c. Cross site scripting
    d. Buffer overflow

37. What type of system replaces rather than repairs components?

   a. Immutable system
   b. Mutable system
   c. Race condition
   d. Trusted system
   e. SoC

38. A company has built a guest Wi-Fi network. Which of the following people could benefit from this new network? Select ALL that apply.

   a. Visitors
   b. Customer services
   c. System administrators
   d. Script kiddies
   e. Employees at lunchtime

39. A security team want to be notified immediately if anyone's account has a higher level of privilege. Which of the following is the BEST way to achieve this?

   a. Least privilege
   b. Permissions audit and review
   c. Continuous monitoring
   d. Security auditing

40. Which of the following can be used by obfuscation?

   a. Race condition
   b. XOR
   c. Input validation
   d. Buffer overlap
   e. Immutable system
   f. Code signing

41. A company wishes to test a new application without impacting any of the current infrastructure. What should the company use to test the application?

   a. Snapshot
   b. Production
   c. Staging
   d. Sandboxing

42. A company has its headquarters in New York and has opened a new branch office in Miami. These two offices need to have a secure connection so that they can transfer data between the sites daily. Which of the following technologies is the MOST cost-effective?

    a. Site-to-site VPN
    b. Lease line
    c. Fiber connection
    d. TACACS+

43. Following a recent audit, the CEO has written a new policy to make the network more secure. The systems administrator followed the policy by implementing secure controls. What type of controls have been implemented? Select the BEST answer.

    a. Administrative control
    b. Control diversity
    c. Technical control
    d. Risk mitigation
    e. Physical control

44. Which of the following can capture motion and provide non-repudiation?

    a. Tape recorder
    b. Camera
    c. SIEM
    d. SoC

45. Which of the following is an example of a SCADA system? Select ALL that apply.

    a. Waterworks
    b. Oil refinery
    c. Bakery
    d. Supermarket

46. A systems administrator has to install full disk encryption on all of their laptops. What piece of hardware is required before FDE can be installed?

    a. SLE
    b. TPM
    c. SoC
    d. ICS
    e. MDM

47. A company has bought a huge department store that they will convert into a data center. They are looking at controlling access to everyone who enters the data center. Which of the following are the BEST to implement? Choose two.

      a. HVAC
      b. Mantrap
      c. Proximity card
      d. Guards
      e. SIEM
      f. CCTV

48. Interpol are investigating criminal activity between London, Paris, and New York. They launch raids on the criminals simultaneously and collect evidence. Now, they want to obtain a much clearer picture of the lines of communication between the criminals. What should they adopt?

      a. Time offset
      b. Normalization
      c. Chain of custody
      d. Memorandum of understanding
      e. Evidence log updates

49. A project manager has stated that each stage of the project should be completely finished before moving onto the next stage. What model is he adopting?

      a. Scrum
      b. Agile
      c. Waterfall
      d. Big Bang model

50. The auditor has carried out an audit of the company's servers and noticed that all of the email servers are located inside the LAN. The mobile sales team have all of their emails on a server known as `Mail1`. The auditor recommended that `Mail1` needs to be isolated from the other mail servers. Which of the following is the BEST solution?

      a. Place it in its own subnet
      b. Attach it to an 802.1x managed switch
      c. Air gap the mail server
      d. Place the mail server in the DMZ

Cheat Sheet

The cheat sheet is a condensed format of the main facts that you need to know before taking the exam. We must learn the exam concepts and not just the answers to a bank of questions.

Frameworks and Guides

- Regulatory: Legally enforceable
- Non-regulatory: Not legally enforceable
- Industry-specific: Ensures compliance for that industry
- Vendor guides: How to set up devices/software

Defense in Depth

- Multiple controls: If one control fails, the next control prevents attacks.
- Vendor diversity: When you have the same product from two vendors, if one fails, you are still up and running.
- Control diversity: Use of more than one control, for example, administrative and technical controls working together.

Secure Network

- DMZ: Boundary layer
- Extranet: Web server residing in DMZ that can be accessed via username and password
- Air gaps: Isolating a system from the network
- NAT: Hides the internal network
- Honeypot: Finds attack methods so that they can be mitigated
- Guest Wi-Fi: Used by guests or employees at lunchtime
- VLAN: Created on a switch, segments the local network, reduced broadcast domain
- VPN: Site-to-site, always-on mode, can be used instead of a lease line
- VPN: Secure connection network from a remote location to work
- VPN concentrator: Sets up a secure session

- SSL VPN: Uses a SSL certificate
- SIEM system: Real-time monitoring, uses a correlation engine
- SIEM system: The wrong input filter produces a false positive

- Load balancer: Manages a high volume of web traffic
- Firewall/DDoS mitigator: Prevents DDoS attacks

Secure Mobile Device

- Screen locks
- Strong password
- Full device encryption: Requires a TPM chip
- Printer/MFD: Can be attacked and is the network interface

Applications

- Whitelist: Allowed applications and their EXE files or DLL binaries
- Blacklist: Banned applications
- Application not running: 99% of time, add to whitelist
- Hardened operating system: Has no vulnerabilities

IoT Devices

- Change username and password immediately
- Prevent connecting directly to the internet
- Difficult firmware updates

Software Development Life Cycles

- Waterfall: One stage finishes before the next stage begins
- Agile: Can start multiple phases, similar to scrum, customer satisfaction paramount

- Staging: Testing with production data, roll back changes before moving to production
- White box pen tester: Test application for vulnerabilities

Embedded Systems

- SCADA network, water purification, oil and gas refineries
- IoT: Refrigerator, wearable technology, home automation
- HVAC: Regulates temperature using hot and cold aisles
- Camera systems: Captures motion, provides non-repudiation, deterrent and detective controls

Secure Application Concepts

- Stored procedure: Sealed script as the best way to prevent SQL injection attacks.
- Input validation: Controls input, prevents SQL injection, buffer and integer overflow attacks.
- Baseline: List of applications before and after to see changes. Only method to detect zero-day attacks.
- Obfuscation: Masks or obscures code.
- Steganography: Hides data inside other data.
- Sandboxing: Isolates applications for testing and patching if they are dangerous.

Cloud Models

- Elasticity: Pay for the amount of resources you use, easily adjustable
- Private cloud: Single-tenant, which means more control
- Public cloud: Multi-tenant
- Community cloud: Same industry sharing the cost of resources

Cloud Services

- IaaS: Desktops, servers, switches, firewall, or pbx
- IaaS: Install OS, patch and configure it – more control
- SaaS: Lease bespoke application – no customization
- PaaS: Hosts your applications – you manage and customize
- SECaaS: Identity management

Cloud Miscellaneous

- VDI: Isolated desktop for contractors or employees
- CASB: Enforces policies for cloud clients

Virtualization

- Type I hypervisor: Bare-metal, Hyper V, ESX, Zen
- Type II hypervisor: Install on an OS, for example, Oracle Virtual Box
- Host: Hosts virtual machines, needs fast disk space, CPU cores, and RAM
- System sprawl: Host/guest running out of resources
- Guest: A user's virtual machine
- Containers: Isolated guest
- Sandboxing: Isolated application for testing, patching, or because it is dangerous
- Chroot Jail: Linux sandbox
- Snapshot: Used for rolling back guests, fastest backup
- VM sprawl: Unmanaged guest
- VM escape: Attacks the host

Resiliency and Automation

- Master image: Produces a consistent baseline
- Non-persistent configuration: Can be rolled back
- RAID 5: Single parity and can lose one disk, 3-32 disks
- RAID 6: Double parity and can lose two disks
- Continuous monitoring: Alerts you immediately
- Snapshots: Virtual machines revert back to an earlier state

Physical Security Controls

- Security guards: Check the identification of people, prevents access
- HVAC: Regulates temperature using hot and cold aisles
- Protected distribution: Protects cables
- Conduits: Protect cables
- Faraday cables: Prevents emissions of data and wireless leaving or entering a network
- Cable locks: Prevent the theft of mobile devices
- Mantrap: Prevents access to buildings or data centers
- Screen filters: Prevents shoulder surfing
- Key management: Prevents keys being taken away overnight and from being cut

4
Identity and Access Management Practice Tests

One of the crucial areas in IT security is controlling access to computer systems to ensure that only authorized people should have access. For the CompTIA Security+ exam, we must be able to compare and contrast identity access management concepts such as identification, authorizing, and accounting with an AAA server. We also need to understand the different types of access, such as something you know, such as a password and pin; something you do, such as swiping a card; and something you have, such as a token. Creating authentication environments such as federation services are heavily tested.

The second area that is tested in the Security+ exam is all about installing and configuring identity services such as LDAP, Kerberos, TACACS+ not RACACS+, CHAP, PAP, MSCHAP not MMSCHAP, RADIUS, SAML, Open ID Connect, OAuth, secure, and NTLM. Next, we will look at different access controls models, such as MAC, DAC, ABAC, and role and rule-based access controls. There are also physical and biometric access controls, followed by access token and certificate-based authentication.

Last but not least, we'll look at different accounts such as user, admin, guest, generic, service, and privilege account and the scenarios when each of these should be used. We need to understand general concepts, such as least privilege, off-boarding, time and day restrictions, standard naming conventions, and account reviews. Then, we need to look at account policy enforcement such as password history, length, complexity, reuse, account lockouts, disabling accounts, and account expiry.

Practice Test 13 – Open Questions – Identity and Access Management

Start off by answering the questions that you have the knowledge base to answer, then on a separate list write down the questions that you do not know the answers to, because you need to revise those areas before testing:

1. What type of access management controls are used for classified data?

2. What is the Microsoft authentication method that uses tickets?

3. What are the three main components of identity and access management? Place them in the correct order.

4. What are the three main components of an AAA server?

5. What are the TCP-based and UDP-based AAA servers? Name three.

6. What is the directory services protocol that stores objects in X500 format?

7. What type of access management control is used for the whole company or department?

8. What type of access management control is used for a subset of a department to complete a subset of duties?

9. What type of account would someone need if they worked in finished goods?

10. What type of account makes it impossible to audit or log an individual user?

11. What type of authentication model can accept the wrong information yet authenticate the user?

12. What is the most common authentication factor that is rejected if entered incorrectly?

13. What is inserted at the identity portion of identity access management?

14. What happens at the authorization portion of identity access management?

15. What is inserted at the authentication portion of identity access management?

16. Explain why a RADIUS or TACACS+ server uses accounting.

17. What type of identity access management control uses cookies to authenticate users?

18. When we log into a website such as Airbnb and we are asked to enter our Facebook account details for authentication, what type of authentication model are we using?

19. When using biometric authentication, how is the crossover error rate measured?

20. What tools should we use to prevent someone from using CD/DVD drives as well as setting up the password policy for the whole domain?

21. What is a third-party to third-party authentication model that uses extended attributes?

22. What is an open source third-party to third-party authentication model that uses extended attributes?

23. What is a third-party to third-party authentication model that uses extended attributes and connects through a WAP?

24. What authentication protocol can be subject to a pass-the-hash attack and what two methods can be used to prevent the attack? Put them in order, with the best solution first.

25. When we access the company network, we need to insert four sets of credentials to access resources. What type of identity and access management concept would make accessing these resources simpler?

26. What type of authentication and access management concepts does gait come under?

27. What type of authentication and access management concepts does your birth date come under?

28. What type of authentication and access management concepts does an elegant natural signature come under?

29. How many authentication factors do password, pin, and birth date amount to?

30. How many authentication factors do iris, retina, fingerprint, and palm come under?

31. What type of authentication and access management concepts do a password and token fob come under?

32. What type of authentication and access management concepts do a password and TOTP come under?

33. What type of identity and access management biometric characteristics does a security guard possess?

34. What type of biometric factors will allow false information to be accepted so that someone can gain access to a system?

35. What type of identity and access services replaced NTLM and prevents a pass-the-hash attack?

36. What type of authentication has the authenticator send a challenge that is used by the person logging in to encrypt their password?

37. What type of authentication is used during **Point to Point** (**PPP**) authentication where the password is sent in clear text?

38. What type of Microsoft authentication is seen as being mutual authentication, single sign-on, and is time-dependent?

39. What type of authentication can be device or location-based dependent?

40. What type of authentication system is XML-based and can be used between third parties?

41. What type of authentication system can be used between third parties using extended attributes? What are extended attributes?

42. What type of authentication system is used between third parties using extended attributes where the connection method is using a wireless connection?

43. How can we measure that the biometric authentication system is reliable?

44. My company has decided to use shared accounts for the customer services department. What problems might this cause an auditor in relation to monitoring or auditing?

45. Two Scottish people get into an elevator in New York that is using voice recognition technology and don't seem to be able to get the elevator to work. What should the systems administrator have done when setting up the elevator?

46. What type of user should be allocated a privileged account?

47. What type of certificate-based authentication can only be used by military personnel?

48. My smart card expired a month ago and a new card was issued; however, when I try to access data that I encrypted six weeks ago, I cannot access it. What actions are required to access the data?

49. An IT consultant is setting up a new Active Directory domain for a company that has 200 users. What is the most simplified method of setting up accounts when you do not wish to use smart cards?

50. When someone leaves a company, what are the responsibilities of the HR and IT teams?

Practice Test 14 – Fill The Gaps – Identity and Access Management

Fill-the-gaps questions really test your knowledge base, and can be quite vague at times. In the CompTIA Security+ examination, some of the test questions can also be quite vague, hence the value of this section.

Complete the answers that you can, then make a list of those topics that you are getting wrong, as you need to revise these areas before you take the test. Best of luck.

In the following questions, fill in the gaps to make the statement. Each underlined section of the sentence represents one word—for example, _____ means that one word is missing; _____ _____ means that two words are missing:

1. Each individual needs a _____ account to be able to access the company's network for business purposes.

2. _____ _____ _____ is an access control model based on the classification of data.

3. A _____ account is required by system administrators or service technicians.

4. A password, pin, or birth date are single factors and come under the category of something you _____.

5. _____ is used by an AAA server for logging access to a database that can track user access.

6. An example of _____ _____ _____ is using NTFS file permission to access data.

7. _____ is a form of authentication where the credentials are transmitted in cleartext.

8. When EAP-TLS is used for _____ authentication, the administrator needs to install a _____ on the host device.

9. London and Paris are both single factors and come under the category _____ you are.

10. _____-_____ authentication can be based on the location of the end user.

11. _____ services use third-party to third-party authentication with extended attributes and _____, which is XML-based authentication.

12. A _____ _____ is an example of a very popular form of multifactor authentication.

13. _____ authentication prevents replay attacks as it uses USN and _____ stamps.

14. _____ comes after identification and authentication and sets out the access level a user has.

15. _____ and _____ are both AAA servers that provide authentication, authorization, and accounting. _____ is an AAA server that uses EAP.

16. _____ uses tokens for authentication and can be used with _____ __ _____, which can use Facebook accounts to authenticate the individual.

17. _____ is used for authentication and is where the server sends a challenge string to the end user, who uses this to _____ their password.

18. Where users need multiple user accounts to access multiple applications, this process can be simplified by using _____ _____ __, which requires only one set of credentials.

19. _____ creates, stores, and manages objects such as a user, group, or printer in a directory service. It can also be used to search for user accounts. A more secure version is _____, which uses TCP port 636.

20. _____ _____ _____ _____ is a granular access control method that uses a value that's unique to that user.

21. Gait is the way that you walk and comes under the category of something you _____.

22. _____ _____ _____ _____ can be applied to a subset of a company or department who carries out a subset of duties.

23. _____ is where a user inserts their _____ card or a _____ and comes before authentication and authorization.

24. A _____ _____ enables access by swiping the card or placing it near the reader.

25. A _____ _____ is a multifactor access control card that works in conjunction with a PIN.

26. An iris scanner is a _____ device that's used for biometric purposes.

27. _____ _____ _____ will prevent an authorized user from gaining access to a system.

28. One of the major factors of how accurate your biometric authentication is looking at a low value of the _____ _____ _____.

29. _____ is a time-based password that has a time limit of 30-60 seconds that expires on first use; however, _____ has no time limit but also expires on first use.

30. _____ _____ are used by departments but prevent auditing or monitoring to an individual user.

31. When a company employs temporary workers, we have different shift patterns and want to enforce access when they are on the clock. This can be done by introducing _____ ____ ____ _____.

32. _____ _____ _____ will prevent an authorized user from accessing a system.

33. When an employee leaves a company, the HR department should conduct _____ _____, while the IT team need to enforce the ____-_____ policy to ensure that all the computer equipment has been returned.

34. _____ _____ _____ is used to structure the creation of user accounts and computer accounts.

35. _____ _____ is achieved by ensuring that passwords contain a mixture of lowercase and uppercase characters, numbers, or special characters that are not used in programming.

36. To ensure that employees within a company have the correct access levels to the systems, an auditor will carry out periodic _____ _____ and reviews.

37. _____ is an open source federation service that uses cookies.

38. The security administrator needs to ensure that _____ _____ and _____ _____ are enforced to protect a user's account details from being reused by a hacker.

39. _____ _____ should be adopted to ensure that users are not accessing data that they don't require for their job role.

40. When a user has a different username but multiple passwords to access multiple websites, they could use _____ _____ to store the passwords so that they don't need to remember them.

41. When a company doesn't use account lockout, the best way to increase the compute time for brute-force attacks is to _____ the length of the user's password.

42. A _____ _____ can be used when applications are installed and need a higher level of privilege.

43. As an additional level of security, a _____ _____ can be used for civilian employees, whereas a _____ card can be used by military personnel.

44. An easy way to prevent employees from inserting USB flash drives or a DVD ROM into desktop computers is to create a _____ _____.

45. _____ _____ _____ _____ can be applied to a whole company or the whole department.

46. A pass-the-hash attack can be prevented primarily by using _____ authentication, which uses tickets, or by simply _____ NTLM authentication.

47. When a network administrator purchases a new wireless router, they should change the default _____ and _____ immediately.

48. When a contractor has a new account created, an _____ _____ should be configured so they cannot work beyond the period of the contract.

49. The data _____ is responsible for classifying data, while the _____ stores it and the _____ gives access to it.

50. TACACS+ and RADIUS are AAA servers. An 802.1x or VPN server are AAA clients who need a _____ _____ so that they can join the AAA environment.

Practice Test 15 – Drag and Drop – Identity and Access Management

I suggest using two different-colored pens: blue or black for answers that are easy for you to identify and a red or different-colored pen for answers that you are unsure of. This way, you can identify your strong and weak areas.

Place the answers into the relevant answer boxes in the following table, starting with the answers that you can easily identify. Make a list of those that you cannot answer on your first time through, as you need to revise those areas. Then use logic to answer the remaining questions.

Insert the phrases at the end of this section into the appropriate answer boxes in the following table. Each phrase can only be used once:

Description	Answer
What uses port 1813?	
What comes after identification during access management?	
Two policies that affect BYOD.	
Something you do.	
Differentiate between different items in a report.	
What uses TCP port 49?	
Control access for a whole department.	
Two accounts that have higher than user privilege.	
What type of device is an iris scanner?	
What type of authentication is company A and company B?	
Prevents a single user from accessing the system once they have finished work.	
This is done prior to leaving a company.	
Something you know.	
Where password policies are set up.	
A password with a 30-60 second time limit.	
What is third-party to third-party authentication using extended attributes that connect using a wireless connection?	
Controls access for a subset of duties and a subset of a department.	
Lets you authenticate using your Facebook account and its protocol.	
Access management based on file classification; for example, a secret.	
Who gives access to classified data?	
Something you have.	
Who stores classified data?	
Who is the person who decides the classification of a document?	
Location-based authentication.	
Access based on department or location.	

Use the following options to answer the preceding questions:

Authentication	RADIUS federation	MAC	ABAC	Exit interview
Password and PIN	Custodian	RADIUS accounting	Open ID Connect, OAuth	Owner
Context-aware	TOTP	Standard naming convention	Token fob, read proximity card	Administrator
Group policy	Rule-based access control	Signature, gait	Role-based access control	TACACS+
Federation	AUP, on-boarding	Physical	Time-of-day restriction	Privileged, service

Practice Test 16 – Mock Exam 4

Start off the mock exam with a clean sheet of paper and note down the questions that you cannot answer or are guessing at, because you need to revise those areas. When you take this test, follow these instructions:

DOs:

- Read the questions carefully; do not scan. Draw diagrams on questions you are unsure of.
- Rule out the wrong answers to leave the correct answer.
- When you narrow the answers down to two possible answers, you have a 50–50 chance of being right. Read the question again and look for the finer details that will give one of those options a 60–40 chance of being right.
- Flag up for review (in the top-right of the screen) the questions that you don't like. Do not answer them, as the review screen will show those items in red. Don't waste time trying to work them out at this stage.
- Before ending your review, go down the columns from left to right and ensure that all questions have an answer.
- At the end, check all of the questions' answers and finish the exam.

DON'Ts:

- Scan through the questions, especially if English is your first language
- Second-guess yourself
- Change answers
- Reread the whole exam if you have spare time

Answer the following questions:

1. A network administrator is placing a new VPN server on a multinational network and his job ticket has the following information:

```
Shared Secret    2hi23kdofpdsmd779kghmjmtju
```

What is the purpose of this shared secret? Choose the BEST option.

a. It is the password so that the VPN can become a RADIUS client
b. It is the admin password for the VPN server
c. It is a hash of the admin account for the VPN server
d. It is a SHA-1 hash value

2. Which of the following fall under the category *something you do*? Select all that apply.

a. Password
b. Natural signature
c. Token
d. Handwriting
e. Gait
f. Tap
g. Swipe
h. Birth date

3. A hacker has visited the website of a multinational corporation where he obtained the names of the CEO Frederick Deeks and CFO Steven Young. A log file from the SIEM system shows his attempts to log into the company's network:

```
09:00 FrederickDeeks invalid credentials
09:01 FDeeks invalid credentials
09:02 DeeksF invalid password
09:03 DeeksF invalid password
09:04 DeeksF account locked out
09:05 YoungS invalid password
09:06 YoungS invalid password
09:07 YoungS account locked out
```

What method has the hacker used for his attack? Choose the MOST suitable answer.

    a. Brute force
    b. Dictionary
    c. Social engineering
    d. Standard naming convention

4. Two of London's top universities are joining forces in a joint venture where students will move between universities. They will not merge the accounts domains but will need an authentication model that they can both participate in. All students will connect via 4G wireless routers. Which of the following authentication models is the MOST suitable for them to use?

    a. Federation services
    b. Kerberos
    c. Single sign-on
    d. Wireless federation
    e. RADIUS
    f. RADIUS authentication

5. The security administrator is carrying out an annual audit of the classified documents to see whether or not the classifications should be downgraded. Which of the following entities should he consult?

    a. Custodian
    b. Data owner
    c. Administrator
    d. Steward

6. The CEO has tasked the IT director to buy a new biometric access system that will be resilient as the current system is rejecting attempts by authorized users. Which of the following measurements should interest the IT director?

    a. False acceptance rate
    b. Compatibility with current systems
    c. Crossover error rate
    d. False rejection rate

7. Which of the following authentication environments uses cookies?

    a. Kerberos
    b. OAuth
    c. WPA2-PSK
    d. Federation services

8. A toy company has temporary workers who are working for them for two weeks prior to Christmas. They work three different shift patterns so that the company has additional labor to cover all 24 hours in a day. What are the BEST ways for the systems administrator to set up these accounts? Choose two.

    a. Complex password
    b. Password history
    c. Account expiry
    d. Time and day restrictions
    e. Account lockout

9. The cyber security administrator notices that the customer services department are using shared accounts. Which of the following activities will be hindered by these accounts? Choose the two MOST suitable activities.

    a. Brute force attacks
    b. Accurate auditing
    c. Monitoring
    d. Password changes
    e. Group policy objects

10. A young graduate was given a games console at his graduation party. The next day, he went to Thailand on a holiday with university friends. The graduate decided to stay in Thailand for six months. When he arrived home, he opened his games console and entered a password that was designed for single use. What type of authentication was the games console using?

    a. Password authentication
    b. Token-based authentication
    c. TOTP authentication
    d. HOTP authentication

11. The systems administrator needs to roll out an identity and access management system that is user-based. Which of the following controls is the BEST for the systems administrator to adopt?

    a. MAC
    b. Role-based access control
    c. DAC
    d. Rule-based access control

12. One of the United Kingdom's top banks has decided to increase the security of online payments over £1,000. When payments are over £1,000, the bank will send a short-lived verification code to their mobile telephone. What type of additional authentication is being used?

    a. Federation services
    b. OTP
    c. HOTP
    d. Kerberos
    e. Single-sign on
    f. OAuth

13. A multinational organization is using usernames and passwords for new users until they obtain a smart card and PIN, which is the primary authentication method. How many factors of authentication is the company using in total?

    a. A single factor
    b. Two factors
    c. Three factors
    d. Four factors

14. A doctor's surgery has found out that some senior employees have been accessing the medical records of famous clients and selling their information to the press. What could the company have done to prevent this? Chose the BEST answer.

    a. Use auditing and review
    b. Permissions auditing and review
    c. Use a SIEM system to log security events
    d. Monitor access to data using group policy

15. According to security bulletins, there has recently been a rise in the number of brute-force attacks. What should the security administrator use to prevent the company from being attacked?

    a. 18-character passwords
    b. Complex passwords
    c. Account lockout
    d. Password history with a value of 25

16. An audit has found that biometric devices are allowing outside personnel to access the computer systems. Which of the following BEST describes what the audit has found?

    a. FRR
    b. FAR

c. CER

d. All of the above

17. Which of the following is XML-based? Choose two.

a. Kerberos

b. Directory services

c. OTP

a. SAML

b. Smart card

18. Which of the following is the AAA server that uses EAP?

a. DIAMETER

b. TACACS+

c. 802.1x

d. RADIUS

19. Your company is running the IT computer systems and services for the Olympic games and needs to have some additional IT technicians from an agency to work on a site in London. What is the BEST type of account that these technicians should be given so that they can fulfill their duties?

a. Guest account

b. Privileged account

c. Service account

d. User account

20. Which of the following authentication environments uses tokens?

a. Kerberos

b. OAuth

c. WPA2-PSK

d. Federation services

21. Which of the following fall under the category *something you have*? Select all that apply.

a. Gait

b. PIN

c. Voice

d. Token

e. Iris

22. A multinational corporation has offices in New York, Paris, Tokyo, and London. The company uses group-based access control. However, there are different policies that are related to the different locations. What is the best way for the security administrator to set up access control so that only those people in the respective locations can see data related to their site?

     a. MAC
     b. RBAC
     c. DAC
     d. ABAC

23. A multinational corporation spans seven different countries and a remote access policy for each site that follows the following criteria:

- They can log into their own location
- Data must remain within their own countries
- They cannot log into any other location

Which of the following is the MOST appropriate authentication method for them to use?

     a. Kerberos
     b. RADIUS
     c. Federation
     d. Context aware authentication

24. The marketing department have a group called `mktgp1` that contains all the members of the department. This group has full control access to the marketing data folder. The marketing department has three interns working for them over the summer months and wish them to have read-only access to the marketing data. Which of the following methods would be the most appropriate to achieve this? Select all that apply.

     a. Add the interns to `mktgp1`
     b. Create a new group called interns
     c. Create individual accounts for the interns
     d. Create a shared group for the interns
     e. Add the interns to the group called interns
     f. Give read access to the marketing data to the interns group

25. You are the systems administrator for a company that makes kitchenware. Your company is now being computerized and you need to give accounts to those employees that work in dispatch so that they can print off labels and enter the date that all the items were picked up on by the postal service. What type of account is the MOST suitable account for these employees?

> a. Privileged account
> b. Service account
> c. User account
> d. Guest account

26. In a multinational corporation, only the CFO, David Lloyd, and his deputy, Mark Birch, are allowed to authorize payments. What type of authentication does the system administrator need to adopt?

> a. Kerberos authentication
> b. Rule-based authentication
> c. Separation of duties
> d. Group-based authentication
> e. Role-based authentication
> f. Federation services

27. The systems administrator has been tasked with setting up a new password policy to reduce the possibility of someone guessing an employee's password. He has to ensure that users cannot keep using the same password and to make those passwords as secure as possible. Which of the following should the system administrator adopt? Choose two.

> a. Account lockout
> b. Password history
> c. Account expiry
> d. Simple passwords
> e. Complex passwords

28. Which of the following is the BEST tool to set up the password policy for a directory services environment?

> a. Credential manager
> b. Directory services
> c. Whitelisting
> d. Group policy

29. Which of the following are AAA servers? Select all that apply.

    a. IAS
    b. RADIUS
    c. Credential manager
    d. Federation services
    e. TACACS+

30. Employees at a large multinational company based in London use smart cards to access their desktops and laptops. The cyber security administrator has just rolled out new smart cards. Each door now has a card reader where the smart card can be swiped to allow entry and exit. Which of the following BEST describes why the new smart card can be used in this way?

    a. The chip on the smart card allows access
    b. The smart card doubles up as a proximity card
    c. The smart card doubles up as an access token
    d. To prevent the user leaving the smart card in their computer for security reasons

31. Which of the following authentication protocols can be subjected to a pass-the-hash attack?

    a. Kerberos
    b. SAML
    c. OTP
    d. HOTP
    e. NTLM

32. Which of the following authentication environments uses tickets?

    a. Kerberos
    b. OAuth
    c. WPA2-PSK
    d. Federation services

33. Which of the following is the AAA server that works in conjunction with a directory service?

    a. IAS
    b. TACACS+
    c. Kerberos
    d. RADIUS

34. Which of the following authentication methods use single sign-on? Select all that apply.

    a. Proximity cards
    b. Kerberos
    c. Federation services
    d. Group policy

35. What type of information will you input during the identification stage of identity and access management? Choose all that apply.

    a. Smart card
    b. PIN
    c. Username
    d. Token
    e. Password

36. A new sales person called Ariadne plugged her laptop into the company network and spread a virus that caused damage to the main servers. What policy does the IT manager need to write to prevent a reoccurrence of this?

    a. Least privilege
    b. Acceptable use
    c. Off-boarding
    d. On-boarding
    e. Remote access

37. Lawyers working in the legal department handle trade secrets on a daily basis. Which of the following is the MOST secure way for them to access the system?

    a. Complex passwords
    b. Five-character passwords
    c. Random generated passwords
    d. Eight-character passwords

38. When someone is logging into a domain environment, what is the correct sequence to follow?

    a. Identification, accounting, authentication, authorization
    b. Authentication, identification, authorization
    c. Identification, authentication, authorization
    d. Identification, authorization, authentication
    e. Accounting, identification, authentication

39. What type of information will you input during the authentication stage of identity and access management? Choose all that apply.

        a. Smart card
        b. PIN
        c. Username
        d. Token
        e. Password

40. A cyber security administrator is setting up a RADIUS server for accounting and logging it to a SQL database. What is the purpose of accounting in relation to identity access management? Choose the BEST answer.

        a. Log the type of authentication protocol being used
        b. Ensure that the user inserts the shared secret
        c. Tracking users' actions for billing purposes
        d. Log the method of user identification
        e. Log the user's access levels

41. The IT director has informed the systems administrator that all sales personnel will only be able to use the systems between 8 am and 5 pm, Monday to Friday. What type of access control model would be the MOST suitable for the systems administrator to adopt?

        a. Federation services
        b. Rule-based authentication
        c. Group-based authentication
        d. Role-based authentication

42. John Smith has been looking for hotel accommodation for his holidays, but the prices were very expensive. Then, he went onto the Airbnb website and found a reasonably priced property to rent. He had never used Airbnb, so he created a new account. However, they asked him to verify his identity using his Facebook account. What type of authentication method is the Airbnb website using?

        a. OAuth
        b. Facebook authentication
        c. Open ID Connect
        d. Web-based authentication

43. The **Chief Executive Officer** (**CEO**) has asked a systems administrator to help him reorganize his laptop. One of the major problems that the CEO has is that he cannot remember his passwords for the following accounts:

- Facebook
- Instagram
- Gmail
- Hotmail
- Yahoo

What can you do to make the life of the CEO easier with the least amount of administrative effort? Select the BEST choice and select ALL that apply.

    a. Put them all in a group and assign him permissions for the group
    b. Use a credential manager
    c. Put them on his favorites in the web browser
    d. Have a Notepad document on his desktop where he can cut and paste the password
    e. Use Open ID Connect

44. When users are changing departments, their old accounts have been known to be used by personnel in the old department, sometimes giving them more access to data than they should have. What is the BEST way to prevent this from happening in the future?

    a. Delete the old account immediately
    b. Usage audit and review
    c. Set up a SIEM system for real-time monitoring
    d. Weekly permission audit and review

45. The United States military are using an embedded card that is accompanied with a PIN for authentication. What type of card are they using? Select the correct answer.

    a. PIV card
    b. Smart card
    c. Proximity card
    d. CAC card
    e. Mastercard

46. A systems administrator is tasked with setting up least privilege for all the members of staff for the forms library folder, which is located on a Linux server. Which of the following is the BEST way for him to set this up?

    a. --- rwx ---
    b. rwx --- ---
    c. rwx rwx rwx
    d. --- --- r—

47. The company help desk have raised tickets all morning, where the authorized company personnel who have inserted the correct information have been refused access to the system. Which of the following BEST describes what fault has occurred?

    a. Smart card
    b. FAR
    c. Username and password
    d. FRR

48. What two actions should the systems administrator take when someone leaves a company?

    a. Delete the user's account
    b. Inform the HR department before the exit interview
    c. Disable the user's account
    d. Reset the password or PIN
    e. Inform the HR department after the exit interview

49. Which of the following will increase the compute time for a brute-force attack? Select the MOST appropriate answer.

    a. Account lockout
    b. 14-character password
    c. Complex passwords
    d. Long password reuse
    e. Eight-character password

50. What type of factor authentication is a smart card and PIN?

    a. Single factor
    b. Dual factor
    c. Two factors
    d. Multifactor

Cheat Sheet

The cheat sheet is a condensed format of the main facts that you need to know before taking the exam. We must learn the exam concepts and not just the answers to a bank of questions.

Authentication Factors

- **Something you know**: Password, PIN, birth date
- **Something you are**: Iris, retina, fingerprint, palm, voice
- **Something you do**: Swipe, gait, signature
- **Somewhere you are**: Location, London, Poland
- **Single factor**: All from the same group
- **Dual factor**: From more than one group

Federation Services

- Third-party to third-party authentication
- Uses extended attributes
- **SAML**: XML-based
- **Shibboleth**: Open source using cookies
- **RADIUS federation**: Federation services connecting via wireless

AAA

- RADIUS: UDP port 1812
- RADIUS accounting port 1813
- DIAMETER: Upgrade of RADIUS using EAP
- TACACS+ - Cisco AAA: TCP port 49
- RADIUS accounting: Logs and tracks users

Authentication Types

- Kerberos: Uses tickets, prevents replay and pass-the-hash attacks
- OAuth: Uses tokens
- Federation services: Uses cookies
- Open ID Connect: Uses a Facebook or Google account and needs OAuth
- Context-aware: Based on location

Account Types

- User: For employees
- Service: For applications
- Privileged: For service technicians and administrators
- Generic/default: Change immediately
- Identity: Smart card or username
- Authentication: Password or PIN
- Authorization: Access levels

Account Policy Enforcement

- Password history: Prevents reuse of a password
- Password length: The longer the better; increases the compute time for brute-force attacks
- Complexity: Three from uppercase, lowercase, numbers, and special characters not used in programming
- Account lockout: With low value prevents brute-force attacks
- Account expiry: Required for the length of the employee's contract

Access Control Models

- MAC: Based on classification, the owner gives classification and the administrator gives access
- DAC: NTFS permissions
- ABAC: Based on a user's attributes
- Role-based access control: Subset of the department, a subset of duties
- Rule-based access control: Applies to the whole organization

Physical Access Control

- Smart cards
- Proximity cards
- Tokens
- TOTP: Needs a device to display code

Biometrics

- FAR: Allows unauthorized access
- FRR: Prevents authorized access
- CER: Where FAR and FRR are equal; low value shows working well

General Concepts

- Least privilege: Allocates only the rights for the job role
- Off-boarding: Claims back company equipment
- Exit interview: Carried out by HR to determine the reason for leaving
- Standard naming convention: Structure for new accounts, printers, and computers
- Permission auditing and reviews: Ensures employees have the correct level of permissions

5

Cryptography and PKI Practice Tests

As an IT professional, securing data and devices is part of the day-to-day workload. You need to be familiar with the PKI infrastructure. You need to know about the CA structure including the Intermediary CA, CRL, OCSP, renewing certificates, whether to use public or private certificates, and how to distinguish each of these. You will need to know when to choose SAN certificates over the wildcard certificates as well as the role of the Key Escrow and the Data Recovery Agent.

The exam will measure cryptography concepts including symmetric and asymmetric encryption, stream and block cipher, and which concept is better for transferring a large amount of data. You must know the impact of different key lengths and ephemeral keys. A security analyst needs to know when to use hashing, salting, obfuscation, and steganography and how to secure data in use or in transit. Good knowledge of cryptographic algorithms and their characteristics is required to obtain the Security+ Certification.

As an IT professional you must know how to install and configure wireless devices and know the different wireless cryptographic protocols and authentication methods.

Practice Test 17 – Open Questions – Cryptography and PKI

Start off by answering the questions that you have the knowledge base to answer, then on a separate list write down the questions that you do not know the answers to, because you need to revise those areas before testing:

1. A university professor has started a lesson on how encryption works. What was the format of the data input and what was the format of the encryption output?

2. The CEO has asked me to purchase a single X.509 that can be installed on several servers in the same domain and once installed, it will have those servers' names on the certificate. What type of certificate do I need to purchase?

3. A captain in the Army encrypted data five years ago with his old CAC card. Last week, he obtained a new CAC card; why can he not decrypt the old data?

4. After Bill has received the encrypted data from Ben, he wants to send an email to Bill saying that the data has been received. He decides to digitally sign the email so that it cannot be tampered with in transit. What key does he need to use for this purpose?

5. What two things do digitally signing an email provide?

6. One of the lawyers decides that he needs to encrypt data held on his smartphone; what asymmetric encryption algorithm is the best for him to use?

7. The captain has decided that he needs to encrypt data on his military mobile telephone; should he use the same encryption algorithm as the lawyer in the previous scenario?

8. The account administrator wishes to prevent duplicate passwords being stored and has been advised to purchase a key stretching algorithm by the security administrator. Can you name two tools that he can use?

9. What is the unique identifier that is embedded into the X.509 certificate?

10. What is the purpose of the HSM and what two functions does it provide?

11. Why has the security administrator recommended using a key stretching algorithm and what purpose does it serve?

12. The CEO has been complaining that the company policy documents have been amended without his authority. How can you protect the integrity of these documents?

13. The human resources team wants to protect PII information when it passes between them and the legal team. How can this be achieved?

14. The CEO has asked you to explain to him how hashing is used and he wants you to recommend two algorithms. What should you explain to him?

15. The CEO want to know if hashing is reversible. What should you tell him?

16. You are the cybersecurity analyst for a large organization and a new intern is completing his assignment for college; he asks you to explain to him what a POODLE attack is. What can you tell him?

17. What is the purpose of **Diffie Hellman Ephemeral** (DHE) and **Elliptic Curve Diffie Hellman Ephemeral** (ECDHE)?

18. The CEO has just purchased a new high-speed laptop and has asked you how can he best protect the data on the laptop. What should you tell him?

19. Now that you have protected the data on the CEO's laptop, he brings in his mobile telephone and asks you to protect the data-at-rest on his phone. What will you do?

20. The web administrator rings you to ask whether you can protect the data-at-rest on a backend server that works in conjunction with the company website. What should you implement?

21. You are going to build an internal **Certificate Authority** (**CA**). When you build the CA, what is another name for the master key that is created?

22. Your company wants to use their own certificates for 1,000 users, rather than purchasing them from an expensive external supplier. What type of certificates do you need?

23. The company sales people have been guilty of leaving removable devices such as USB drives in hotel rooms and the CEO has asked you to provide a solution that will mitigate the risk of data theft should this happen in the future. What type of solution will you recommend?

24. Your company sells goods to the B2B community. What type of certificates are required to ensure that the customers will make purchases?

25. Your company security team always takes the company CA offline when not in use. What is the reason for this?

26. Who is the person that designs and builds the CA and the intermediary authorities?

27. The cybersecurity team wants to secure the CA against compromise or someone creating fraudulent certificates. What should the cybersecurity team use to complete this task?

28. In a Public Key Infrastructure environment, who is responsible for the signing of the X.509 certificates?

29. Two different companies, each with their own PKI infrastructure, want to be able to provide cross-certification between each other. What type of trust needs to be in place?

30. Steven and Fred wish to encrypt data between themselves and have decided to use PGP. What type of trust does PGP use?

31. The security administrator is going to use FDE on the company laptops to protect the data-at-rest. He needs to ensure each laptop either has a TPM chip on the motherboard or an HSM. What trust model will be adopted for the FDE?

32. The IT manager has asked you how can you tell that a certificate is valid if you do not have any internet access. What can you advise him?

33. The PKI administrator has informed you that users are complaining that certificate validation is going slow. How can you improve this situation?

34. The web developer is creating a new website and wants you to describe to him what certificate stapling is. What should you tell him?

35. You are the security administrator when the CEO calls you and asks what the process of obtaining a new certificate is called. What should you tell him?

36. You have applied for the position of Key Escrow; what do you know about the functionality of the Key Escrow?

37. The secret service needs to encrypt an extremely large amount of data before archiving it. What type of encryption would be best for them to use?

38. What is the function of the Data Recovery Agent, what data does he recover, what tools does he need, and where can he obtain them?

39. The security administrator has a certificate and wants to know the three ways that it can be identified as a private key?

40. The security administrator has a certificate and wants to know the three ways that it can be identified as a public key?

41. The security administrator has found a certificate in the safe that has been marked as extended validation. What is so special about this certificate and how can I tell the difference between it and a normal certificate when it has been installed?

42. The CEO overheard two of his IT professionals talking about using Diffie Hellman. What can you tell him about this algorithm?

43. The CEO has asked me to purchase a single X.509 that can be installed on several servers using different domain names. What type of certificate do I need to purchase?

44. A developer is writing a new software package and he wants to ensure that customers can verify that the software that they have is a genuine copy and not fake. What action does he need to take once he has written the application?

45. What is the difference between stream and block cipher modes, and which one will you use to encrypt large blocks of data?

46. The security administrator is going to implement a new VPN. What are the strongest and weakest methods of encryption with an L2TP/IPSec VPN tunnel?

47. Bill and Ben are two lawyers who wish to send encrypted data between themselves. What is the first stage of encryption?

48. Bill is going to encrypt data to send to Ben. What key should he use for the encryption?

49. When James and Fred are going to use PGP for encryption between them without a PKI environment, what is the first stage that they need to complete?

50. What do James and Fred need to be able to set up PGP?

51. The X.509 certificate on a web server is coming up with an error, *This certificate is not trusted*. What two things does the security administrator need to check to ensure that the certificate does not give this error?

52. The security administrator has been contacted by the CEO and the CFO, as they want to ensure the integrity of the email that they send between them. What solution will you recommend?

53. The security administrator has been contacted by the CEO and the CFO, as they want to ensure the integrity and confidentiality of any email that they send. What solution will you recommend?

54. What are the five symmetric encryption algorithms in the Security+ syllabus?

55. A network administrator in a PKI environment has captured a key with Wireshark. What type of key has he captured?

56. What type of VPN will use an SSL certificate?

57. A stateful firewall has captured a packet that is normally 2 MB in size but it seems to be 2.3 MB. What type of attack has it identified?

58. A developer wants to ensure that he can mask source code to prevent a competitor from reading it if it is stolen. What technique does he need to adopt?

59. Which of the following symmetric algorithms is faster: Blowfish or Twofish and why?

60. Jane encrypts data to send to Debra who then sends her a reply. Why can't Jane decrypt the message with the key she used to encrypt in the first place?

Practice Test 18 – Fill The Gaps – Cryptography and PKI

Fill-the-gaps questions really test your knowledge base, and can be quite vague at times. In the CompTIA Security+ examination, some of the test questions can also be quite vague, hence the value of this section.

Complete the answers that you can, then make a list of those topics that you are getting wrong, as you need to revise these areas before you take the test. Best of luck.

In the following questions, fill in the gaps to make the statement. Each underlined section of the sentence represents one word—for example, _____ means that one word is missing; _____ _____ means that two words are missing:

1. The _____ key length, the faster it is, but larger the key length, the more _____ it is.

2. Key stretching and _____ are techniques where random characters are _____ to the password to make them harder to crack using brute force.

3. Full Disk Encryption is used to protect data-at-rest on a _____ and Full Device Encryption is used to protect data-at-rest on a _____ _____.

4. _____ is used for encryption on small devices as it has a small key but uses the Diffie Hellman handshake, however, when encrypting data on a military mobile telephone ____- _____ is used.

5. Ephemeral keys are _____ lived keys and the two examples are _____ and _____.

6. The first stage in encryption whether we are using asymmetric or symmetric encryption is to _____ _____.

7. Encryption between two people can be carried out using _____, where no PKI architecture is required.

8. To ensure integrity of data, we will use a technique called _____; two examples of these are _____ and _____.

9. Two key stretching algorithms are _____ and _____. These increase the _____ time it takes a brute force attack to crack a password.

10. HMAC provides both data _____ and data _____.

11. The strongest encryption protocol used by a VPN is _____ and the weakest encryption used by a VPN is _____. They are both symmetric encryption; this means that they use ____ key.

12. When using symmetric encryption, one key is used and this is known as the _____ _____ or the _____ _____.

13. Blowfish is _____ than Twofish as it uses a ____-bit key length whereas Twofish uses a _____-bit key length.

14. When encrypting data, we will use someone else's _____ key and for decryption, they will use the corresponding _____ key.

15. _____ is a technique where we will either mask data or make it difficult to be read should it be stolen.

16. When a data packet is leaving the network and is stopped by the _____ firewall as it is larger than expected, this shows that someone is trying to steal the data using a technique called _____.

17. A technique called a _____ _____ provides integrity of an email; this is where the email is signed using the originator's _____ key, and this also provides non-repudiation.

18. The Data Recovery Agent needs to obtain the user's _____ key to recover their data when their certificates are corrupt and he obtains this key from the _____ _____.

19. Certificate _____ is where the web server bypasses the CRL and goes directly to the _____ for faster validation of the certificate.

20. A private key has a _____ format with an extension of _____, whereas the public key has a _____ format with a _____ format.

21. Certificate _____ prevents fraudulent certificate from being produced and prevents compromise of the CA.

22. The function of the certificate architect is to design the PKI structure and install both the CA and the _____.

23. The Key Escrow manages the private keys for third parties and stores them in a

_____ _____ _____.

24. The _____ _____ shows your certificate and the path from the intermediary who issued the certificate to the CA who signed the certificate. It uses three different layers or a trust error will occur.

25. A _____ _____ is where an attacker tries to match a hash value so that he knows the password.

26. WPA2-Enterprise uses _____ with a _____ server for authentication to a domain.

27. _____ _____ _____ is used to check the validity of certificates, even if you have no internet, but when it goes slow you might adopt an _____ for faster validation.

28. A _____ certificate can be used when one certificate can be purchased for use on multiple servers in the same domain.

29. A _____ certificate can be used when you need to insert multiple domains using a single IP address.

30. A _____ _____ is where two separate PKIs trust each other for cross-certification.

31. _____-_____ is the more secure wireless encryption protocol as it used AES.

32. The certificate serial number is called the _____ and is located on the X.509 itself.

33. _____ is used for wireless connection and is set up by first inserting a _____ then afterward, you access the network by simply pushing a button.

34. When setting up _____-_____ for authentication, a certificate needs to be installed on the endpoint or host.

35. When setting up _____-_____ for authentication, a certificate needs to be installed on the server.

36. When encrypting data, you will use _____ _____ public key and they will decrypt the data with the corresponding _____ key.

37. Asymmetric encryption uses two keys, and these are known as the _____ key and the _____ key and the public key. The _____ key is never given away.

38. A private key has a _____ format and a file extension of .pfx and can be protected by a _____.

39. A public key has a P7B format and a file extension of _____ and _____ be protected by a password.

40. A PEM certificate uses a _____ ____ format.

41. _____ is where we have a small change to plaintext and this results in many more changes to the ciphertext.

42. _____ encrypts data-in-transit; this replaced the legacy SSL protocol.

43. _____ encryption is used to encrypt large amounts of data as it uses a small key with _____ cipher.

44. L2TP/IPSec uses a _____ _____ handshake to create a secure session before the data is transferred. This is known as _____.

45. Six different symmetric encryption algorithms are RC4, ____, _____, _____, Blowfish, and _____.

46. _____ _____ and _____ are methods of email integrity and data integrity.

47. A _____-_____ certificate cannot be validated as it has no method of checking its validity.

48. _____ is a substitution cipher used by Julian Caesar to encrypt his battle plans and prevent his enemies from intercepting them. Each letter is replaced by the ____ letter after it in the _____.

49. A _____ is a random number used once in cryptography.

50. _____ make the relationship between the cyphertext as encryption key as complex as possible.

Practice Test 19 – Drag and Drop – Cryptography and PKI

I suggest using two different-colored pens: blue or black for answers that are easy for you to identify and a red or different-colored pen for answers that you are unsure of. This way, you can identify your strong and weak areas.

Place the answers into the relevant answer boxes in the following table, starting with the answers that you can easily identify. Make a list of those that you cannot answer on your first time through, as you need to revise those areas. Then use logic to answer the remaining questions.

Insert the phrases at the end of this section into the appropriate answer boxes in the following table. Each phrase can only be used once:

Description	Answer
Encrypts large amounts of data	
Asymmetric encryption algorithm	
Encryption for data-in-transit	
Key Escrow holds these for third parties	
Appends random characters to passwords	
Encrypts data-at-rest	
Strongest VPN encryption	
PKI encryption key	
Matching two hashes	
Prevents someone from reading code	
List of precomputed hashes	
Web server bypassing the CRL and going direct to the OCSP	
A short-lived key	
Used for encrypted data-in-transit	
Key stretching algorithms (select two)	
Private key is a P12 format, .pfx extension protected by a ...	
Stage 1 when building a CA, you need to choose between	
Prevent CA compromise and creation of fraudulent certificates	
Hashing algorithm	

Where the certificate serial number is located	
Make an application for a new certificate	
Creates a secure session for a L2TP/IPSec VPN	
Check certificate validity when you have no internet	
Certificate that can be used for multiple hosts, same domain	
Certificate that can be used across multiple domains and have details such as the IP address inserted	

Use the following options to answer the preceding questions:

Salt	Password	SAN certificate	Wildcard	Symmetric encryption
Public key	RSA	FDE	Private keys	Ephemeral
CRL	Obfuscation	Diffie Hellman	AES	Certificate pinning
Collision	Rainbow table	Certificate stapling	MD5	OID
FDE	TLS	Bcrypt, PBKDF2	CSR	Public or private, CA

Practice Test 20 – Mock Exam 5

Start off the mock exam with a clean sheet of paper and note down the questions that you cannot answer or are guessing at, because you need to revise those areas. When you take this test, follow these instructions:

DO:

- Read the questions carefully; do not scan. Draw diagrams on questions you are unsure of.
- Rule out the wrong answers to leave the correct answer.
- When you narrow the answers down to two possible answers, you have a 50–50 chance of being right. Read the question again and look for the finer details that will give one of those options a 60–40 chance of being right.
- Flag up for review (in the top-right of the screen) the questions that you don't like. Do not answer them, as the review screen will show those items in red. Don't waste time trying to work them out at this stage.
- Before ending your review, go down the columns from left to right and ensure that all questions have an answer.
- At the end, check all of the questions' answers and finish the exam.

DON'T:

- Scan through the questions, especially if English is your first language
- Second-guess yourself
- Change answers
- Reread the whole exam if you have spare time

Answer the following questions:

1. You are the security administrator for a large company and you need to install a certificate on a host. Which type of wireless authentication are you intending to implement?

    a. PEAP
    b. EAP-TTLS
    c. EAP-FAST
    d. EAP-TLS

2. The sales manager has problems with his laptop and decided to clear the SSL cache. What will the impact of this be?

    a. He will get a certificate trust error.
    b. His browser will operate using TLS as SSL has been removed.
    c. It will roll back the user password and he will be unable to log in.
    d. The laptop's search performance will increase.

3. Which of the following uses a unique username and password to access a wireless access point?

    a. WPS
    b. PSK
    c. WEP
    d. RC4

4. What type of keys are held by the Key Escrow?

    a. Public keys
    b. Private keys
    c. Session keys
    d. Shared keys

5. A company has just installed an 802.1x managed switch that will authenticate the devices. What needs to be installed on the device so that it can be authenticated?

    a. A unique MAC address
    b. A valid certificate
    c. A static IP address
    d. All of the above

6. In a PKI environment, who is responsible for issuing certificates to users?

    a. Certificate architect
    b. CA
    c. OCSP
    d. Intermediary authorities

7. An internal auditor has established that the company is spending too much money on X.509 certificates for internal devices and has recommended the cheapest certificate that can be used internally with the least administrative effort. The cybersecurity analyst is against this certificate being implemented as it poses a security risk. Which of the following certificates has the auditor recommended?

    a. PEM
    b. Public certificate
    c. Code signing certificate
    d. Self-signed certificate

8. David Lloyd obtained a new certificate for his smart card in March of this year. He needs to access data that he had encrypted in February but is getting an error denying access. What does he need to do to be able to decrypt the old data?

    a. Obtain a copy of his old public key to decrypt the data
    b. Obtain a copy of the session key to decrypt the data
    c. Obtain a copy of his old private key to decrypt the data
    d. Use his current public key to decrypt the data
    e. Use a copy of his current private key to decrypt the data

9. An administrator needs to set up a wireless access point that fulfills the following criteria:

- Uses a password on installation
- Can be subjected to a brute force attack
- Accesses the WAP by pushing a button

    a. CCMP
    b. PSK

  c. WPS

  d. TKIP

10. If two individuals are going to implement PGP to encrypt emails, what are the first two stages that they need to complete?

  a. Obtain public and private key pair

  b. Establish a CA

  c. Establish a web of trust

  d. Exchange public keys

  e. Exchange private keys

11. Two different companies are launching a joint venture and they want cross-certificate authentication. What type of trust is being implemented?

  a. Web of trust

  b. Federation services

  c. Hardware root of trust

  d. Trust model

12. A company wishes to install a wireless access point to use WPA2-Enterprise. Which of the following is a requirement? Choose two.

  a. RADIUS federation

  b. RADIUS server

  c. WPS

  d. EAP-TLS

  e. 802.1x

13. Which of the following certificate types uses a Base64 format?

  a. DER

  b. CER

  c. PEM

  d. PFX

14. A multinational corporation purchases two companies, Company X and Company Y. Neither of these companies will not merge but need to be set up for authentication using SAML and extended attributes. When an employee from Company Y comes into Company X, they will connect via a wireless access point using WPA2-Enterprise. What type of authentication model is being adopted?

  a. Single sign-on

  b. Kerberos

c. Federation services
d. RADIUS authentication
e. RADIUS federation

15. What would a security administrator implement to prevent a CA compromise?

a. Certificate chaining
b. Certificate stapling
c. Certificate pinning
d. Certificate signing request

16. A bank is going to obtain a certificate for its online banking to assure customers that it has a higher level of trust. What type of certificate has a higher level of trust?

a. Domain validation
b. Domain trust certificate
c. Extended validation
d. Enhanced validation

17. A network administrator is examining a packet trace and he notices a packet containing a `.cer` extension and a format of P7B. What type of information has he captured?

a. Private key
b. Public key
c. Shared key
d. OID

18. Which of the following encryption methods uses a single key? Select three.

a. RSA
b. SSL
c. TLS
d. SHA-1
e. DES
f. Twofish
g. AES

19. A financial institution has just installed a public certificate on their online banking website. After installation, the background went green when the URL was inserted. The IT director explained that this was because the certificate had a higher level of trust. What type of certificate has just been installed?

a. SAN certificate validation
b. Private Key validation

c. Extended validation

d. Wildcard certificate validation

e. Server certificate

20. Which of the following wireless authentication protocols does not need a certificate to be installed and provides mutual authentication?

a. EAP-TLS

b. EAP-FAST

c. EAP-TTLS

d. PEAP

21. Which of the following encryption methods use a short-lived key? Select two.

a. DES

b. DHE

c. RSA

d. ECDHE

22. What is the name of the key that is used by the Certificate Authority to sign the X.509 certificates?

a. Private key

b. CA key

c. Public key

d. Root key

23. The website administrator has been complaining that the certificate validation is extremely slow and the customers are facing issues. In order to rectify the situation, the security administrator has pointed the web server to the OCSP, bypassing the CRL for certificate validity. What is the technique that he just implemented?

a. Certificate pinning

b. Certificate stapling

c. Certificate chaining

d. Key Escrow

e. Data Recovery Agent

24. A network administrator is analyzing the network traffic and has discovered an item called the OID. What type of technology is the packet associated with?

a. ICMP traffic

b. Certificates

c. Encryption

d. Hashing

25. The FBI apprehended a well-known hacker who has been in possession of a document that has a list of passwords with the relevant hashes using MD5 format. It is 680 GB in size; what is the name of this document?

a. Hashing table

b. Collision table

c. Red table

d. Rainbow table

26. A security administrator expanded the Certification Path tab of a certificate and he notices the following information:

```
Digicert Global Root 2
Digicert Global CA 2
www.securityplus.training
```

What does the preceding output represent?

a. The root CA

b. Certificate pinning

c. Certificate stapling

d. Certificate chaining

27. The network administrator is setting up a L2TP/IPSec. What mode should be used for the IPSec session?

a. GRE encapsulation

b. Transport mode

c. Tunnel mode

d. SSL mode

28. A cyber security administrator discovers that a certificate that is being used on 50 web servers has been compromised. What action needs to be taken to rectify the situation using the least amount of administrative action?

a. Certificate pinning

b. Certificate revocation

c. Certificate chaining

d. Certificate stapling

29. The company has used the same legacy wireless access point for 15 years and it has now stopped working. The company needs to replace it. What type of wireless access point should be purchased?

    a. WPA – TKIP
    b. WEP
    c. WPA2
    d. WPA2 – CCMP

30. The network administrator has requested a VPN certificate for a branch office. A new IT administrator purchased a SSL certificate because it was discounted. Although this certificate is legacy, what type of VPN can he now install?

    a. L2TP/IPSec
    b. SSL VPN
    c. PPTP VPN
    d. He cannot use the certificate at all

31. What is the purpose of a security administrator using a technique called obfuscation?

    a. Hiding data inside other data
    b. Masking data to prevent it from being read
    c. Encrypting data
    d. Hashing data

32. Which of the following tools will make it difficult for a brute force attack to crack a password? Select two tools.

    a. Obfuscation
    b. Bcrypt
    c. PBKDF2
    d. XOR
    e. RSA
    f. SHA1

33. Mary wants to ensure integrity of an email she is sending to Robert; what protocol should she use for the emails?

    a. TLS
    b. IMAP 4
    c. S/MIME
    d. POP 3

34. The Chief Information Officer wants to ensure that the integrity of data on the financial data folder can be maintained. Which of the following cryptographic algorithms will be used? Select two.

    a. Encryption
    b. MD5
    c. Obfuscation
    d. SHA1
    e. CBC
    f. XOR

35. The cybersecurity administrator wishes to prevent duplicate passwords being stored; therefore, he is using a technique that appends a random value to the password. What is he implementing?

    a. Salting
    b. XOR
    c. Steganography
    d. Obfuscation

36. A company wants to encrypt emails between its three mail servers. Which protocol should they use?

    a. TLS
    b. IMAP 4
    c. S/MIME
    d. POP 3

37. The website developer has been tasked with purchasing the most cost-effective certificate to fulfill the following:

    • One certificate can be used on twenty web servers.
    • When installed on each web server, the certificate name becomes unique.

Which of the following certificates should be purchased?

    a. SAN certificate
    b. CER certificate
    c. Code signing certificate
    d. Wildcard certificate
    e. Server certificate

38. The network administrator has been tasked by the CEO to ensure that data-in-transit is as secure as possible. Which of the following algorithms will he select?

      a. DES
      b. SSL
      c. TLS
      d. PAP

39. Mary wants to encrypt the emails she sends to Carol. What protocol should be used to encrypt the emails?

      a. TLS
      b. SSL
      c. PGP
      d. SHA1

40. A system administrator is going to install a user certificate on a sales person's laptop. What is the first stage that he needs to carry out?

      a. Ensure the laptop has a TPM chip.
      b. Enable a rule on the host-based firewall for the new certificate.
      c. Obtain a certificate from the Key Escrow.
      d. Initiate a CSR.

41. A company is going to set up a guest wireless access point for visitors and employees at lunchtime. How should the wireless access point be set up for each group? Choose two.

      a. Open system authentication for visitors
      b. Open system authentication for employees
      c. WPA2-Enterprise for employees
      d. WPA2-Enterprise for visitors

42. David Lloyd contacted the help desk as he cannot access his encrypted data because his key is corrupt. The help desk is going to escalate the problem: who should they contact and what is needed to decrypt the data? Where can they obtain it from? Choose three; each provides part of the solution.

      a. System administrator
      b. David Lloyd's public key
      c. Key Escrow
      d. Custodian
      e. David Lloyd's private key
      f. Data Recovery Agent
      g. David Lloyd's shared key

43. Bob has arrived at Brussels airport and he connects to the wireless network; it notifies him that he is connected. However, when he tries to access the internet, he cannot access it. What seems to be his problem?

        a. Too many people are using the Wi-Fi.
        b. He is in a Captive Portal.
        c. He needs to enable a rule of his device's firewall.
        d. He is too far away from the wireless access point.

44. A multinational organization wants to increase the time it would take for a brute force attack to crack a user's password. The IT manager has said that the company should purchase two key stretching algorithms to fulfill this task. What of the following should the IT team purchase? Choose two.

        a. Obfuscation
        b. Bcrypt
        c. Nonce
        d. PBKDF2

45. A notorious hacker is typing a password into a notepad document; he saves it and hashes the document with SHA1. What type of attack is he carrying out?

        a. Substitution cipher
        b. Pass-the-hash attack
        c. Rainbow table attack
        d. Collision attack
        e. Brute force attack

46. A new cybersecurity intern has been asked to fetch the CEO's old private key so that he can decrypt some old data. How will he identify a private key? Select two.

        a. P7B
        b. P12
        c. P13A
        d. .cer
        e. .pfx
        f. .pem

47. A security administrator is buying a certificate for the company that can fulfill the following:

- Multiple domain names can be inserted.
- An IP Address can be inserted.
- A DNS server can be inserted.

Which of the following certificates should be purchased?

    a. SAN certificate
    b. CER certificate
    c. Code signing certificate
    d. Wildcard certificate
    e. Server certificate

48. A company needs to encrypt 1 TB of data as quickly as possible. What type of encryption should they use?

    a. Elliptic Curve Cryptography
    b. Asymmetric encryption
    c. Symmetric encryption
    d. RSA

49. The cybersecurity administrator has been tasked with protecting data stored on the sales teams' laptops. What should the cybersecurity administrator install or configure to ensure that the laptop is capable of protecting the data? Choose two.

    a. UEFI chip
    b. TPM chip
    c. USB 3.0
    d. Full Disk Encryption (FDE)
    e. Asymmetric encryption
    f. Symmetric encryption

50. A company is going to use IPSec to encrypt data between the finance server and members of the finance team. What mode should be used with the IPSec?

    a. Interconnection security mode
    b. Tunnel mode
    c. Split tunnel mode
    d. Transport mode

Cheat Sheet

The cheat sheet is a condensed format of the main facts that you need to know before taking the exam. We must learn the exam concepts and not just the answers to a bank of questions.

Certificate Hierarchy

- CA has a root key
- Stage 1—do you want to install a public or private CA
- Public CA required for trading on the internet (B2B)
- Architect builds the CA and intermediary authorities
- Intermediary authorities issue the certificates
- Certificate pinning—prevents CA compromise and fraudulent certificates

Certificate Validation

- **Certificate Revocation List** (**CRL**)—checks certificate validity
- OCSP—used only when the CRL is going slow
- Certificate stapling—when the web server bypasses the CRL and goes directly to the OCSP

Private Keys

- Always retained—never given away
- P12 format, `.pfx` extension, password protected
- Used to decrypt data
- Used to digitally sign email—provides integrity
- Key Escrow—holds the private keys for third parties
- **Hardware Security Module** (**HSM**)—stored and manages the keys for the Key Escrow
- **Data Recovery Agent** (**DRA**)—obtains private keys from the Key Escrow to recover data

Public Keys

- Used to encrypt data—normally use someone else's to send encrypted data to them
- Exchange with others
- P7B format or `.cer` extension

Trust Models

- Two different PKIs trusting each other—bridge root of trust
- PGP—uses a web of trust
- TPM—hardware root of trust

Miscellaneous

- **Object Identifier** (**OID**)—unique numerical value equivalent to a serial number
- PEM—Base64 certificate
- Extended validation—higher level of trust, green background when used
- Certificate chaining—three levels showing the vendor, CA, and computer installed on
- Wildcard certificate—used for multiple servers in the same domain, also used by host headers
- **Subject Alternate Domain** (**SAN**)—used for multiple domain names
- **Certificate Signing Request** (**CSR**)—application for new certificates

Cryptographic Algorithms

- Encryption—asymmetric or symmetric—exchange keys
- Stream cipher—encrypt one bit at a time
- Block cipher—encrypt blocks of data

Symmetric Encryption

- Single key—private or shared key
- Encrypts a large amount of data
- Encrypts data-at-rest
- DES—56 bits
- 3DES—168 bits
- AES—up to 256 bits
- Blowfish—64 bits
- Twofish—128 bits

Asymmetric Encryption

- Two keys—public and private
- Diffie Hellman—create a secure tunnel
- RSA
- Elliptic curve—used for small devices
- PGP—encryption between two people
- TLS—data-in-transit

Ephemeral Key

- Short-live—one-time use
- **Diffie Hellman Ephemeral (DHE)**
- Elliptic curve **Diffie Hellman Ephemeral (DHE)**

Hashing

- Provides data integrity
- SHA1 160 bits
- MD5 128 bits

- Hash before and after—data integrity produces the same hash
- Rainbow tables—precomputed password and associated hashes
- Collision attack—two hash values match

Key Stretching

- Increases compute time for brute force attacks
- Key stretching tools—bcrypt, PBKDF2

Basic Cryptographic Concepts

- Obfuscation—masks data so it cannot be read if stolen
- Steganography—embeds or hides data inside other data
- Salting—appends a random value to passwords
- Salting—prevents duplicate passwords being stored
- Salting—reduces the effectiveness of a brute force attack
- Data-in-transit—use TLS or VPN to protect it
- Data-at-rest—use encryption such as AES/DES/3DES
- Data-in-use —resides in volatile RAM.
- Key strength—smaller the key size the faster but less secure it is

Wireless Security – Low to High

- WEP—very weak
- WPA—backward-compatible with WEP
- WPA2—CCMP—strongest wireless encryption—uses AES
- WPA2—enterprise—RADIUS with 802.1x for domains
- PSK—press shared key
- TKIP—legacy
- WPS—push button to activate, insert password first

- WPS and PSK—can be subject to brute force attack
- Disable SSID—can be discovered by a wireless packet sniffer
- Troubleshoot Wi-Fi—use wireless packet sniffer/scanner
- Site survey—needed before setting up WLAN

Wireless Authentication

- Guest Wi-Fi—used by visitors or employees at lunchtime
- Open system authentication—no security
- Captive portal—request secondary information to connect
- EAP-TL—certificate on the endpoint
- EAP-TTLS—certificate on the server
- EAP-FAST—mutual authentication, no certificate
- PEAP—encapsulates EAP packets, uses TLS

6
Risk Management

Most companies will have a cybersecurity team to deal with the increasing amounts of cyber crime and one of the key areas that they will adopt to protect the company is risk management.

In this chapter, we will first look at the importance of policies, plans, and procedures that need to be in place to help to protect an organization. We will look at standard operating procedures, agreement types, personnel management including background checks, exit interviews, NDA, and general security procedures.

Next, we will look at Business Impact Analysis concepts such as RTO, RPO, MTTR, and MTBF followed by the impact of mission essential functions, single point of failures, and the impact of disaster recovery.

A security IT professional needs to know about risk management processes and concepts. They need to know the different types of threat actors, how the complete risk registers, and different risk assessments such as qualitative and quantitative. Good knowledge of the different types of penetration testing and how it differs from vulnerability scanning is essential. We need to evaluate risk by looking different aspect relating to cost such as SLE, ARO and ALE. BIA needs to look at RPO/RTO.

Once the professional knows the theory behind risk assessment, they need to look at their ability to respond to incidents, by invoking the various incident response plans and procedures. When dealing with incidents, the security professional needs to know the basic concepts of forensics such as order of volatility, collecting evidence, and implementing chain of custody.

Lastly, the sanitizing and destruction of different types of data from paper waste to the removal and destruction of hard drives and classified and unclassified documents is crucial to ensure that hardware items that are disposed of and do not contain any company data.

Before you begin with each set of tests, you need to keep a sheet of paper, so that areas that you get wrong and are guessing at are written down. This is so that you identify the weak areas that you need to revise before testing.

After the test, there is a *Cheat sheet* section, with a summary of the most relevant information that you need; you must know each of these facts 100%.

Practice Test 21 – Open Questions – Risk Management

Start off by answering the questions that you have the knowledge base to answer, then on a separate list write down the questions that you do not know the answers to, because you need to revise those areas before testing:

1. An auditor has established that an aircraft company will be able to operate for 3 hours without their online ticket sales. What has the auditor measured?

2. The IT manager has been logging the number of failures of the video-conferencing application. What technique have they been using?

3. In a risk management scenario, why are the MTTR and the RTO similar?

4. If the risk management team is using a qualitative risk assessment, what grading system will they use to measure this?

5. If the risk management team is using a quantitative risk assessment, what are they measuring?

6. In a manufacturing environment, a bolt snapped on one of the major pieces of equipment, resulting in the loss of 20 production hours. What Business Impact Analysis concept has just occurred?

7. When measuring Business Impact Analysis, what is the most critical factor?

8. What is the most critical task that the human resources department must carry out before they appoint a new employee for the finance department?

9. When someone leaves the company why does the human resources department carry out exit interviews?

10. Bill and Ben have decided to go into partnership with each other. They will draw up a business partnership agreement. What details are in this agreement?

11. What type of agreement should I take out with Hewlett Packard so that I can have them maintain my printers? How would this agreement be measured?

12. When I outsource my printers to Hewlett Packard, what type of risk treatment am I fulfilling?

13. What is the difference between an MOU and MOA?

14. You are a risk consultant who visits a new customer to advise them of the risks that they have and how those risks should be treated. What is the first stage in risk assessment?

15. The financial director is very suspicious of Mary, the payments clerk within the finance team. Your company is going to employ a financial consultant to investigate the situation; what is the first action that the financial director needs to take to facilitate this inspection?

16. At the end of each day, everyone in the sales team takes all of the documents and notepads that they have been using and locks them away each evening. What technique are they using and why?

17. Who is the person who classifies data in a **Mandatory Access Control** (**MAC**) environment?

18. What is the purpose of a company hiring a data custodian and are they allowed to give access to data?

19. Your company has lost 10 members of the IT team because they have won the lottery, therefore, you need to hire contractors from a recruitment agency. What type of account should be allocated to the contractors?

20. What is the first stage that an external penetration tester needs to ensure to establish before the testing begins?

21. Ariadne, the top salesperson for the company, has decided to bring her home laptop into the company as a BYOD device. The first day that she brought it into work, she spread a virus to the network and infected a domain controller and a file server. What precautions should have been taken to avoid this from happening?

22. What is the purpose of the CEO if a company is writing a job rotation policy?

23. Prior to the cashier sending out payment to creditors the checks are double-checked by the financial director who also countersigns the checks. What is the purpose of this?

24. Your company has had a meeting with all of the departmental heads and they have discussed introducing a company-wide risk register. What is the purpose of this register and how often should this register be reviewed?

25. Why would a company adopt risk avoidance strategy as the treatment for a risk?

26. The IT team has decided to outsource the IT support for their Skype environment; what type of risk treatment is this and why would it be adopted?

27. What is a technical control that is used to reduce risk? Name two of these controls associated with purchasing a new laptop.

28. The IT manager of a Scottish-based company has refused to insure the company premises against hurricanes and tornados. Why has he done this and what type of risk treatment has he adopted?

29. The company auditor has been inspecting the IT team and has discovered that since the IT policies were written, a new technology has been born that makes the company vulnerable. He reports this to the CEO. What are the two options that the CEO could undertake to mitigate the risk of using the new technology?

30. What is the purpose of a Standard Operation Procedure?

31. During the risk assessment, what is the purpose of an SLE, ARO, and ALE and how do they interact with each other?

32. John Smith sent out an email to the whole company advertising his holiday caravan was for hire in the summer months, using his corporate email. What type of policy has he violated?

33. A police forensics investigator is about to analyze a laptop belonging to a well-known criminal. What are the first and second stages that they needs to carry out to prove to the courts that they have not tampered with the data during investigation?

34. A police forensics investigator is about to analyze an external hard drive belonging to the CEO of a multinational financial company. What are the first and second stages that they need to carry out to prove to the courts that they have not tampered with the data during investigation?

35. What is the purpose of a chain of custody and how is it affected when a detective has collected so much evidence that he must lock the evidence in a suitcase that he puts in the hold when traveling back to his base by aircraft?

36. A member of the finance team is under investigation by the FBI. The FBI has told the company that this individual should not be alerted and their mailbox should be put on legal hold. Can you explain what approach has been adopted?

37. If the cybersecurity team discovers a web-based attack, what is the first step they should take and why?

38. If the cybersecurity team discovers a rapidly expanding virus on the local network, what is the first step they should take and why?

39. If the security administrator discovers that one of the computers is being used a member of a botnet, what is the first action he should take?

40. What is the purpose of the record time offset when collecting data for an investigation and how could it then be used?

41. In a virtual environment, what is the purpose of snapshot before and after a major upgrade?

42. What is the fastest physical backup concept and why?

43. What is the most expensive disaster recovery site to use and why?

44. What is the cheapest disaster recovery site to use and why?

45. In a disaster recovery and continuity of operations, can you explain the principle of data sovereignty and its restrictions?

46. If your company is backing up data using backup tapes, what is one of the most important factors that they must adopt?

47. What type of disaster recovery site would be best for a business selling theater tickets?

48. What would be the benefit of using a cloud-based disaster recovery site?

49. What would be the cheapest type of disaster recovery site and what would be the limitations of using such a site?

50. Explain the concept of risk.

Practice Test 22 – Fill The Gaps – Risk Management

Fill-the-gaps questions really test your knowledge base, and can be quite vague at times. In the CompTIA Security+ examination, some of the test questions can also be quite vague, hence the value of this section.

Complete the answers that you can, then make a list of those topics that you are getting wrong, as you need to revise these areas before you take the test. Best of luck.

In the following questions, fill in the gaps to make the statement. Each underlined section of the sentence represents one word—for example, _____ means that one word is missing; _____ _____ means that two words are missing:

1. When data is being classified, it is the role of the _____ _____ to classify the data.

2. CCTV and motion sensors are _____.

3. Using usernames and passwords instead of a smart card is an example of a _____ control.

4. A _____ _____ _____ is where all paperwork is put into a locked cupboard at the end of the working day.

5. When a new employee is accepted for a position in the finance department, both _____ and _____ _____ are carried out.

6. _____ _____ is when someone takes a holiday so that the company can find out whether fraud or theft has been carried out. ____ _____ is very similar except the workers also gain a new skillset.

7. _____ _____ _____ are step-by-step instructions on how internal tasks should be carried out.

8. _____ _____ _____ measures loss of revenue, purchase of new equipment, and regulatory fines.

9. When someone leaves the company both _____ _____ and _____ _____ should be carried out.

10. On the first day, a new employee is required to sign a ___-_____ _____ to confirm that anything they see as part of their employment is not divulged to any third parties.

11. The _____ _____ _____ measures the amount of time that a company can operate without their data. The _____ _____ _____ is when the company is back to an operational state.

12. _____ _____ _____ _____ measures the reliability of a system as it logs all failures.

13. Should a normal repair take four hours but, on a Friday, takes three hours, this means that the MTTR will _____ and the RTO will _____.

14. _____ __ _____ is where no one person is allowed to complete the whole financial transaction of receiving and paying out money.

15. When a risk is deemed very low and we do not mitigate the risk, this is known as _____ _____.

16. When a risk is deemed to be high and we decide not to participate in the activity, this is known as _____ _____.

17. _____ _____ is where we put procedures in place to reduce risk; this is also known as a _____ control.

18. When a SCADA system has been brought to a halt because one essential bolt has snapped off, this is known as a _____ _____ __ _____.

19. A _____ _____ _____ is made between two parties where one provides a service to the other that is measured in metrics.

20. _____ _____ _____ is made by two parties when they agree on the secure connectivity between each other.

21. A memorandum of understanding is ___ _____ binding; however, a memorandum of _____ is legally binding.

22. A _____ _____ _____ is made by two different parties where they agree about a partnership, who makes decisions, and the roles that each entity fulfills.

23. After disaster recovery, we collect evidence for a lesson learned meeting; collecting this evidence is known as a _____ control.

24. After risk mitigation has taken place, it is not possible to totally eliminate the entire risk; the small amount of risk leftover is known as _____ _____.

25. When destroying a hard drive, the best way is to _____ it, followed by _____, and then degaussing it.

26. The best way to keep data _____ is to encrypt it, therefore preventing anyone from viewing it.

27. _____ _____ _____ prevents PII and sensitive data from leaving the company via email.

28. _____ is the best way to sanitize printed material.

29. A burning bag is used for the destruction of _____ material and a _____ _____ is provided by the company sanitizing the data.

30. _____ ____ _____ details how employees should use the company-owned equipment.

31. In a BYOD environment, two policies that should be adopted are _____ ____ _____ and the ___ _____ _____.

32. Everyone should treat their co-worker with respect and should not threaten or discriminate against them; this is known as _____ ___ _____.

33. Hurricanes, tornadoes, and floods are examples of _____ threats.

34. A foreign government that is well-organized and funded is known as a _____ _____.

35. A threat actor, who has very little programming skills, purchases a program from the dark web; this is known as the _____ _____.

36. The annual loss expectancy is calculated by multiplying the _____ _____ _____ by the _____ ____ __ _____.

37. The first stage of risk assessment is to _____ and classify the _____. This will then determine how you protect and handle it.

38. A _____ _____ is a list of all risks that a company faces. Each risk is owned by the departmental head who will then determine what level of risk _____ should be adopted.

39. When I purchase a new laptop, one of the first pieces of software I install is an anti-virus solution; this is known as _____ _____.

40. When I purchase a new car, I need to insure the car before driving it on the road; this is known as _____ _____.

41. When an auditor has carried out an audit and identifies anomalies, these will be resolved by either writing a new policy or carrying out _____ _____, and both of these are administrative controls.

42. When reviewing disaster recovery procedures, we may carry out a _____ _____.

43. The fastest disaster recovery site is the _____ site, but it is also the most expensive, and the cheapest disaster recovery site is the _____ site.

44. A company has two data classifications called public and private and then introduces two more categories, personal and financial. The reason for introducing the additional categories is for better _____ _____.

45. When sanitizing a hard drive, the best method to use is _____ followed by _____ and then _____.

46. A _____ is a threat actor who will try and steal your trade secret to manufacture your products and beat you to market.

47. A _____ _____ function is one that if it fails, then the entire system will also fail.

48. _____ _____ is where an incident is reviewed after all of the facts on how the incident occurred in the first place so that it can be prevented in the future.

49. Capturing the network traffic during a web-based attack is an example of _____ _____, where the most perishable evidence is collected first.

50. The first stage in disaster recovery is to write the _____ _____ as each incident is different.

Practice Test 23 – Drag and Drops – Risk Management

I suggest using two different-colored pens: blue or black for answers that are easy for you to identify and a red or different-colored pen for answers that you are unsure of. This way, you can identify your strong and weak areas.

Place the answers into the relevant answer boxes in the following table, starting with the answers that you can easily identify. Make a list of those that you cannot answer on your first time through, as you need to revise those areas. Then use logic to answer the remaining questions.

Insert the phrases at the end of this section into the appropriate answer boxes in the following table. Each phrase can only be used once:

Description	Answer
An agreement more than a gentleman's agreement but not legally binding	
Risk treatment—risk too high	
When a system has been returned to an operational state	
Using a username and password when your smart card expires	
How long it takes to repair a system	
The first stage after finding a remote attack	
Used when the auditor has been to visit and finds adverse actions, select two	
Risk treatment—outsourcing	
After taking a system image, next stage	
Number of events per year	
How evidence should be controlled	
Risk—calculating loss	
Loss of a single item	
Fastest physical backup	
Amount of time a system can be down without impacting the business	
Fastest backup	
Risk treatment—risk very low	
After identifying a virus, the next stage, choose two	

SLE X ARO	
Best way to dispose of paper	
Risk—high, medium, or low	
What you will do with the record time offset	
Two ways to dispose of a hard drive	
Prevent data from being deleted	
Risk treatment—technical control to reduce risk	

Use the following option to answer the preceding questions:

ALE	Snapshot	Pulping	Capture network traffic	Acceptance
MOU	Qualitative	Legal hold	Time normalization	Transference
RPO	Full	Mitigation	Avoidance	Quantitative
SLE	Chain of Custody	Hash the data	Shredding, Pulverizing	Quarantine, Isolate
ARO	Shredding, Pulverizing	RTO	Compensating control	MTTR

Practice Test 24 – Mock Exam 6

Start off the mock exam with a clean sheet of paper and note down the questions that you cannot answer or are guessing at, because you need to revise those areas. When you take this test, follow these instructions:

DO:

- Read the questions carefully; do not scan. Draw diagrams on questions you are unsure of.
- Rule out the wrong answers to leave the correct answer.
- When you narrow the answers down to two possible answers, you have a 50–50 chance of being right. Read the question again and look for the finer details that will give one of those options a 60–40 chance of being right.
- Flag up for review (in the top-right of the screen) the questions that you don't like. Do not answer them, as the review screen will show those items in red. Don't waste time trying to work them out at this stage.
- Before ending your review, go down the columns from left to right and ensure that all questions have an answer.
- At the end, check all of the questions' answers and finish the exam.

DON'T:

- Scan through the questions, especially if English is your first language
- Second-guess yourself
- Change answers
- Reread the whole exam if you have spare time

Answer the following questions:

1. The security team in a multinational corporation believes that one of the finance employees was embezzling money from the company. They hired a financial expert who was going to review the situation. Which of the following is the BEST solution for the company to adopt so that they can find out whether or not any criminal activities have been going on?

    a. Have the expert sit in a conference room to audit the financial files.
    b. Use job rotation to move the finance employee to another position.
    c. Use auditing on the company's databases.
    d. Send the employee on holiday by adopting mandatory vacations.

2. The CEO of a multinational corporation is going to write a policy that states the four different levels of access depending on the smart card issued. What type of control is the CEO carrying out?

    a. Least privilege
    b. Compensating
    c. Physical
    d. Administrative

3. Which of the following scans will cause damage to a system?

    a. Intrusive
    b. Non-credentialed
    c. Credentialed
    d. Passive

4. A government has contracted a third-party company that will destroy classified paper documents and provides the government with a disposal certificate. How will the disposal company destroy the documents?

    a. Shredding
    b. Pulping

c. Burning
d. Pulverizing

5. A SIEM system has been used to identify security risks in real time. The system found a vulnerability on a host but when the cybersecurity administrator examined the host, they didn't find any vulnerability. This is known as a false positive. Which of the following are the BEST reasons why this happened? Select two.

a. Time was synchronized every 5 minutes.
b. The wrong host was scanned.
c. The wrong input filter was used.
d. The correct input filter was used.

6. Which one of the following roles will test bespoke applications before they are released to the public?

a. Black box
b. Gray box
c. White box
d. Active reconnaissance

7. Which of the following threat actors are very well organized with plenty of resources available to them?

a. Hacktivist
b. Organized crime
c. Competitor
d. Script kiddie
e. Nation state

8. A risk analyst is looking at information that was recently collected. What type of risk assessment had been carried out?

Product	Probability	Impact	Risk score
A	9	3	27
B	8	3	24
C	7	7	49
D	2	6	12

a. Risk transference
b. Qualitative risk
c. Quantitive risk
d. Risk register

9. Interpol is launching dawn raids in multiple countries against drug lords. They will be collecting evidence to try and find out how the financial transactions are carried out and who is the person running the show. What is the MOST important action that they need to take while collecting the evidence?

      a. Document the evidence
      b. Chain of custody
      c. Bag the evidence
      d. Record time offset

10. What does an auditor need before he performs an audit? What reporting does he do afterward? Select the BEST two options.

      a. He needs the latest policies and procedures.
      b. Stop a policy violation and direct the staff on the latest policies.
      c. He will inform management about his findings recommending change management or a new policy.
      d. He needs the latest standard operating procedures.

11. An auditor is carrying out a risk assessment on the company's mobile telephones, some of which are owned by the employees themselves. The auditor has recommended that the following should be implemented:

- MDM solution
- FDE

Which of the following risks will be mitigated by this implementation? Select all that apply.

      a. Mobile devices will be secure enough to email credit card details.
      b. Mobile devices will be patched and fully hardened.
      c. Data-at-rest will be protected against theft.
      d. Data-in-transit will be protected against theft.
      e. Mobile devices will be centrally managed.
      f. Mobile devices will be protected against theft.

12. Which of the following differentiates MOU and MOA? Choose all that apply.

      a. MOU is a legally binding process.
      b. MOA is a legally binding process.
      c. MOU is a formal agreement between two parties.
      d. MOA is not a legally binding process.

13. The cybersecurity administrator is going to purchase a SIEM system. Which of the following elements are crucial to the selection process? Choose the BEST two.

    a. RPO
    b. RTO
    c. MTTR
    d. MTBF
    e. MTTF
    f. ALE
    g. ARO

14. A cybersecurity analyst has been informed of a web-based attack on the company's file server. What is the FIRST action that the cybersecurity analyst should take?

    a. Disconnect the network interface to prevent the attack.
    b. Start recording the attack methods being used.
    c. Capture the network traffic.
    d. Inform the local police.

15. The British police have come to Spain to extradite a well known criminal back to the United Kingdom. The police handcuff the suspect and pack the evidence into a suitcase that is locked and placed in the aircraft hold. Which of the following have the police not complied with?

    a. Chain of custody
    b. Evidence tampering
    c. Failed to get a receipt for the evidence
    d. Forensic tampering

16. A company suffered a cyber attack and lost $1 million. The CEO has asked that if anyone was involved with the incident, to come forward with the information, so that they can discuss how to prevent an attack in the future. What are they going to carry out?

    a. Lessons learned
    b. Internal investigation
    c. Tabletop exercise
    d. Structured walkthrough

17. The FBI has sent a laptop and external hard drive to the forensics team who will search for evidence. What two things need to be done FIRST by the forensics team?

    a. Hash both of them at the beginning and the end.
    b. Start chain of custody.
    c. Take a system image of the laptop.

d. Take a forensic copy of the hard drive.

e. Make a list of all files on both devices.

18. Prior to an auditor assessing the BIA elements of a multinational corporation, which of the following are the most crucial aspects?

a. MTTR/MTTF

b. RPO/RTO

c. Identification of critical systems

d. Mission-critical functions

19. A company has employed a pen tester to test its security. There have been no details given to the pen tester before he arrived. The systems administrator takes the pen tester into the room where the testing will take place. On the desk are coffee and biscuits and a diagram of network points. What type of pen tester is carrying out the assessment?

a. Black box

b. White box

c. Red team

d. Gray box

e. Green team

20. Which of the following scans will cause the MOST damage to a system?

a. Intrusive

b. Non-credentialed

c. Credentialed

d. Credentialed intrusive

21. Which of the following BEST describes a hot site? Choose three.

a. It is manned and the data is replicated immediately.

b. It is manned and the data is 3 hours old.

c. It is the most expensive site to run.

d. It is the cheapest site to run.

e. It is the best disaster site for B2B.

22. An aircraft was due to take off but one of the refueling technicians noticed that a bolt was missing and alerted the maintenance department. The flight was delayed for over 3 hours while a replacement bolt was found. Which of the following has caused the delay?

a. Failure to carry out safety checks

b. On-boarding was not carried out properly

c. Hardware failure

d. Single point of failure

23. A military site is building a new headquarters with the walls incorporating faraday cages. What are the two main reasons for them choosing this design?

a. It prevents data emissions from escaping.

b. They can use it to lock up laptops.

c. It prevents remote electrical interference.

d. It is used in conjunction with proximity cards.

e. It prevents Wi-Fi from being used internally.

24. A risk analyst is looking at another set of data. What type of risk assessment had been carried out?

	A	B	C
High	Red	Green	Red
Med	Green	Blue	Green
Low	Yellow	Red	Blue

a. Qualitative

b. Probability

c. Avoidance

d. Quantitive

25. There was a tender to provide IT hardware for a military unit and three companies bid for the contract. The cheapest supplier was selected and during the first year of the contract, the hardware was analyzed by the security team as being poor quality and very easy to access. What did the tender process not include? Choose the BEST answer.

a. A background check was not done on the bidders.

b. A supply chain assessment was not done on the bidders.

c. None of the supplier's previous customers was asked their opinion.

d. No quality control documents were requested.

26. The security administrator needs to destroy some paper waste that has been used in a conference. What is the BEST way to dispose of this waste?

a. Shredding

b. Pulping

c. Pulverizing

d. Wiping

27. Which of the following threat actors are most likely to try and steal your trade secrets?

    a. Hacktivist
    b. Organized crime
    c. Competitor
    d. Script kiddie
    e. Nation state

28. A new company employee arrives at the IT department to receive a mobile phone, tablet, and a laptop. Which of the following policies should the new employee abide by? Choose two.

    a. On-boarding
    b. Background check
    c. Job rotation
    d. AUP
    e. Risk register

29. What is the first stage in risk assessment?

    a. Classify the asset
    b. BIA
    c. Risk register entry
    d. Identify the risk treatment

30. The security administrator has found some old hard drives that used to hold company data. Which of the following is the BEST way to sanitize these hard drives?

    a. Shredding
    b. Pulping
    c. Degaussing
    d. Pulverizing

31. Which of the following values do you need to know to establish an ARO?

    a. BIA
    b. SLE
    c. MTTR
    d. ALE

32. A small company has just been informed that their only mail administrator has just found himself another job and will leave the company in two weeks' time. They are now frantically trying to recruit another mail administrator as the cost of hiring a contractor would be too great. Which of the following should they have implemented to avoid this happening? Select the BEST answer.

      a. Separation of duties
      b. On the job training
      c. Job rotation
      d. Mandatory vacations

33. Which of the following should be entered into a risk register? Choose two.

      a. BIA
      b. Risk treatment
      c. Risk owner
      d. Threat

34. An auditor visited a new data center in Galway and made a recommendation that it needed to have a secure and safe environment. Which of the following does the company need to put in place?

      a. Guards of the gate
      b. Proximity card
      c. Guard dogs
      d. Mantrap

35. What type of scan should a systems administrator choose if he wants to identify missing patches, the IP address of the host, and the time and date of the scan?

      a. Passive
      b. Non-credentialed
      c. Credentialed
      d. Incremental

36. Which of the following threat actors are politically motivated?

      a. Script kiddie
      b. Nation state
      c. Hacktivist
      d. Organized crime
      e. Advanced Persistent Threat
      f. Competitor

37. The CEO was informed by the IRS that the new CFO is under investigation by them. The company should take action to prevent him from destroying emails. Which of the following actions did the cyber team adopt?

    a. DLP
    b. SIEM monitoring
    c. Chain of custody
    d. Legal hold
    e. Spam filter

38. A script kiddie is someone with low technical knowledge purchases a program or virus developed by someone else to perform attacks. Where is he MOST likely to obtain the exploit from?

    a. Internet
    b. Intranet
    c. Extranet
    d. Dark web
    e. Best buy

39. Which of the following people are MOST likely to fall victim to a spear phishing attack?

    a. CEO
    b. CFO
    c. Receptionist
    d. Sales person
    e. New intern

40. Which of the following is the BEST way to sanitize these hard drives?

    a. Burning
    b. Pulping
    c. Degaussing
    d. Pulverizing

41. The company is going to carry out a paper-based exercise in the company board room with all of the heads of departments participating. What is this known as?

    a. Administrative control
    b. Management exercise
    c. Structured walkthrough
    d. Table top exercise

42. Which of the following physical backup is the fastest?

     a. Snapshot
     b. Full
     c. Incremental
     d. Differential

43. A company's cyber security team has noticed that a notorious hacker has been on Facebook and Twitter looking at company information pages. What type of action is the hacker carrying out?

     a. Social media attack
     b. Social engineering attack
     c. Active reconnaissance
     d. Passive reconnaissance

44. What type of scan should a systems administrator choose if he wants to identify missing patches, audit files, and look into account information?

     a. Passive
     b. Non-credentialed
     c. Credentialed
     d. Incremental

45. A company in London is opening up a new warm site and has two potential locations, Manchester and New York. The company then selects Manchester over New York. Which of the following information is the MOST crucial reason why New York was not selected?

     a. Links to New York will be slower.
     b. New York and London have different laws.
     c. Backup data cannot be sent to New York.
     d. The currency of New York and London are different.
     e. There is difference power voltage used in the UK and the USA.

46. A cyber security analyst discovers a log file showing the following commands had been executed:

```
Start - run - regedit
C:\ windows\system32\
```

What type of attack has just been carried out?

     a. Passive reconnaissance
     b. Rootkit

c. Backdoor

d. Active reconnaissance

47. A user has lost his smart card and it will take three weeks to get a new card. Which of the following compensating controls can he use in the meantime? Choose the BEST answer.

a. HOTP

b. SAML

c. TOTP

d. Proximity card

48. The company security team have been told that employees are accidentally or maliciously sending out credit card details to entities outside the company. What can they put in place to prevent this from happening in the future?

a. Spam filter

b. Proxy server

c. DLP

d. Least privilege

49. The security administrator had a telephone call from the Chief Financial Officer who believes his computer has a virus. What is the FIRST stage the security administrator should perform?

a. Isolate the computer from the network.

b. Interview the CFO and take a statement.

c. Check the virus log files.

d. Launch a virus scan.

50. Which of the following technical controls will be used to mitigate risk?

a. Mantrap

b. Anti-virus

c. Screen saver

d. Change management

e. ID card check

f. Firewall rules

Cheat Sheet

The cheat sheet is a condensed format of the main facts that you need to know before taking the exam. We must learn the exam concepts and not just the answers to a bank of questions.

Risk Treatments

- Avoidance – risk deemed too high. Avoid activity.
- Acceptance – risk too low – do not mitigate
- Mitigation – reduce the risk; for example, anti-virus on laptop
- Transference – transfer risk to a third party; for example, outsourcing, car insurance

Risk Assessment

- Stage 1 – identify the asset – determine how it is treated and handled
- Quantitative – measurement of loss expressed in a number format
- Qualitative – grading risk as high, medium, or low
- SLE – single loss of an item
- ARO – number of losses in a year
- ALE – SLE x ARO = annual losses in a year
- Residual risk – remaining risk after mitigation

Personnel Management

- Mandatory vacations – employee takes a holiday; the employer discovers fraud or theft
- Job rotation – trains the staff also detect fraud or theft
- Separation of duties – no one person completes the whole transaction
- Exit interview – find reasons for leaving the company
- Off-boarding – returning your company equipment on exit
- **Non-Disclosure Agreement** (**NDA**) – legal agreement to not discuss company business

Business Impact Analysis

- RPO – the amount of time you can be without data, acceptable downtime
- RTO – returning to full operation after a disaster
- MTTR – time to repair
- MTBF – time between failures; measures reliability of a system
- Single point of failure – one item, if it fails, takes the system down

Forensics

- Stage 1 – hard drive – take a forensic copy
- Stage 1 – computer – take a system image
- Order of volatility – collect perishable evidence first
- Record time offset – regional time of evidence that is collected
- Time normalization – putting the record time offsets in sequence
- Chain of custody – who collected and has handled the evidence, should not have a gap
- Rapidly expanding virus – isolate or quarantine immediately

Recovery Sites

- Hot – manned with all data up to date, most expensive site
- Warm – manned data maybe 3 hours out of date
- Cold – water and electricity – no equipment, cheapest site

Data Destruction

- Hard drive – shred first, then pulverize, then degauss
- Paper – pulp first, shred second
- Paper – classified – use a burning bag, obtain destruction certificate

Assessment

Chapter 1: Threats, Attacks, and Vulnerabilities Practice Tests

Practice Test 1 – Solution

1. A polymorphic virus mutates as it replicates, therefore, the hash value will keep changing.

2. A backdoor is put into an application by a programmer so that if the user locks themselves out, they can gain access to the application. A backdoor attack is where they use this password that has been in place since the application was created.

3. The attack here is launched by telephone; therefore, it is a vishing attack.

4. Letting a fireman into your server room is a social engineering urgency attack; if you don't let him in, your building could burn down.

5. This is a disguised ransomware attack; you are parting with money to purchase the full version of the product.

6. A **Remote Access Trojan** (**RAT**) sends passwords to the hacker who then uses them to access your computer system.

7. A zero-day virus can only be detected by using baselines. Day zero is when it is launched and it might take the vendor a few days to find a solution.

8. A logic bomb is a virus that is triggered by an event such as time.

9. Spyware is a stealth attack that secretly tracks your internet usage and habits.

10. Adware uses pop ups as its attack vector.

11. A watering hole attack infects a well-known trusted website.

12. A phishing attack is launched against a manager using email.

13. A spear phishing attack is launched against managers using email. In the exam, ensure you look to see whether it is singular or plural.

14. Employing a third party to incinerate your paper waste prevents dumpster diving.

15. Obtaining an email from the CEO or HR demanding you complete an attached form is a social engineering authority attack.

16. Social engineering consensus is where you want to be accepted as part of a team, so you do what the team does.

17. This is whaling where the CEO clicks on a link.

18. Cross-Site Scripting uses HTML tags and/or JavaScript.

19. An intrusive scan is used during a penetration test and can cause considerable damage to your system.

20. A wireless disassociation attack keeps disconnecting you from your wireless access point.

21. Taking control and sending messages or texts is called Bluejacking; you are basically hijacking the phone.

22. Stealing contacts from a Bluetooth phone is called bluesnarfing.

23. A man-in-the-middle attack is an interception attack where the data is replayed immediately.

24. A replay attack is an interception attack where the data is replayed at a later date.

25. A virus could use port 1900 and a worm could use port 5000.

26. This is a vishing attack where my financial details are obtained via a telephone.

27. This is social engineering tailgating as you have let someone in who has not produced any credentials.

28. This is a social engineering impersonation attack as they pretend to be from your company.

29. This is a botnet carrying out a **Distributed Denial of Service (DDoS)** attack.

30. This is where someone stands behind you in the ATM queue with a camera videoing your transaction; this is a more modern version of a shoulder surfing attack.

31. Inserting too much data into a data field is a buffer overflow attack.

32. A SQL injection attack uses the phrase *1 = 1*. The best form of mitigation is to use stored procedures where the SQL commands are embedded into a script. You would then run the script name. Input validation is another form of mitigation where you control the input.

33. The only way to prevent a DDoS attack is to use a firewall to prevent the attack from reaching the website. You may use a Web Application Firewall or a stateful firewall if your web server is located inside your DMZ. A load balancer cannot deal with DDoS.

34. This is an evil twin where the attacker's WAP looks like the legitimate WAP by using a similar SSID.

35. You can use 802.1x on a managed switch where the legitimate devices use a certificate. This way the 802.1x can validate the device that it lets connect to the switch and rogue devices will be rejected.

36. Jamming is a wireless interference attack.

37. In the CompTIA Security+ exam, if you reinstall an operating system but the virus keeps returning, this is known as a rootkit virus.

38. A computer system that uses NTLM authentication is vulnerable to the pass the hash attack. This can be prevented by using Kerberos authentication or disabling NTLM.

39. A script kiddie is someone who will purchase a program to launch his attack from. A good place to purchase dangerous tools would be the unregulated dark web.

40. A hacktivist is a politically motivated attacker.

41. The most difficult threat actor to detect is the insider threat, sometimes called a malicious insider. He is already inside your network legitimately and therefore is more difficult to track.

42. A competitor is a threat actor who will steal your trade secrets to beat you to market.

43. Pivoting is a technique where you will gain access to a network via a vulnerable low-level host then launch an attack against a more critical computer system such as a SQL database server.

44. A gray box penetration tester knows something about your company network, no matter how trivial it seems.

45. Fuzzing is a technique where random information is submitted to an application to see what information is output. A white box tester does this to see whether any vulnerabilities need to be addressed before putting the application into production.

46. A black box penetration tester is given no information at all. He would try and use a vulnerability scanner to see whether your computer systems have any vulnerabilities that he could exploit. First of all he looks at initial exploitation.

47. Penetration testing is aggressive and penetrates deep into your network and could cause severe damage, whereas a vulnerability scan is passive and identifies missing patches.

48. You would place an end of life HVAC controller into a VLAN to mitigate the risk of attack.

49. The **Chief Security Information Officer** (**CISO**) should write that errors on the customer side should be short and very vague but on the internal side should be long and as detailed as possible to help the support team to diagnose the problem.

50. A monitoring system that does not detect any attacks is known as a false negative.

51. Resource exhaustion is where the CPU usage is running at 100%. You would mitigate this by purchasing a faster processor, installing another processor, or moving some of the load to another server.

52. A smurf attack is an amplification attack launching directed IP broadcasts to the border router. This is a massive amount of ping packets that are seen to be coming from the victim, and this results in the victim getting four times the replies. You can prevent this by disabling IP broadcasts on the border router.

53. A pharming attack redirects you from going to a legitimate website and sends you to a fraudulent website.

54. DNSSEC encrypts the DNS traffic to prevent DNS poisoning attacks. It produces RRSIG records.

55. Session hijacking is an attack where the attacker steals cookies from your computer system.

56. If you type your URL incorrectly, you could be redirected to a fraudulent website; this is known as typo-squatting.

57. Rainbow tables are pre-computed lists of passwords and their corresponding hash values. Rainbow tables are used for collision attacks against passwords stored as hash values.

58. A dictionary attack uses only proper words that you would expect in a dictionary. Any passwords that have random characters or passwords that are misspelled prevent a dictionary attack.

59. A brute force attack is a password attack that uses every available combination of letters and characters. It can be prevented using account lockout with a low value.

60. To prevent duplicate passwords being stored, we would salt them; this would append random characters to the password, making them longer and unique. This is sometimes known as key stretching.

Practice Test 2 – Solution

1. Privilege escalation
2. WPS
3. Active reconnaissance
4. Hoax
5. Servers, end users
6. Birthday attack
7. Replay
8. Security baseline
9. Shimming and refactoring
10. MAC spoofing
11. Non-credentialed
12. Credentialed
13. Authority, urgency
14. Non-intrusive
15. Near field communication
16. End, life
17. False positive
18. Backdoor
19. Passive reconnaissance
20. Faraday cage
21. Default configuration, internet
22. Vendor support
23. Nation State
24. Unauthorized software

25. WEP

26. Organized crime
27. Open source intelligence
28. Input validation
29. Key management
30. Default configurations
31. Weak cipher
32. Persistent
33. WPA2-CCMP
34. Initial exploitation
35. RFID
36. Downgrade
37. Ciphertext
38. Domain hijacking
39. Man-in-the-browser
40. Amplification
41. Brute Force
42. Cross-site reverse forgery
43. Clickjacking
44. Race condition
45. Integer overflow
46. Salting
47. Undocumented assets
48. Untrained users
49. Regression testing
50. Single point

Practice Test 3 – Solution

Description	Answer
The trial software found exploits, but you need to buy the full package	Ransomware
More data is inserted into an application than expected	Buffer overflow
The reason why we shred and burn data is to prevent ...	Dumpster diving
Someone standing behind you records your ATM transaction by using a smartphone	Shoulder surfing
A USB drive plugged into the back of your desktop logs keystrokes	Keylogger

This generates multiple popups	Adware
You have to reinstalled the operating system, but this virus is still there	Rootkit
An attack on the CEO or a high-level executive	Whaling
Someone willing to steal your trade secrets	Competitor
No knowledge or information is given to you	Black-box pen tester
Prevents pass-the-hash attacks	Kerberos
An untraceable virus	Zero-day virus
May cause harm to your system	Intrusive scan
An attack on everyone using a popular trusted website	Watering-hole attack
Complete wireless payment transactions	Near field communication
Obtains a program from the dark web	Script kiddie
Redirects the user to a fraudulent website	DNS poisoning
Listening to a conversation	Passive reconnaissance
The first stage after purchasing an IoT device, change the ...	Default configuration
CPU running at 100% is a sign of …	Resource exhaustion
An email sent to the Board of Directors	Spear phishing
Purchasing fake software from a website	Hoax
An attack using the phrase *1=1*	SQL injection
Hacktivist motivation	Political cause
Prevents SQL injection, buffer overflow, and integer overflow	Input validation

Practice Test 4 – Mock Exam 1 – Solution

1. Answer: a
Concept: This is a social engineering impersonation attack where Joe pretends to be from the help desk. The financial director confirms this.

2. Answer: b
Concept: David Lloyd left exactly 4 weeks ago and logic bombs work on a trigger; here, it was the time of 4 weeks.

3. Answers: c and e
Concept: A pass-the-hash attack needs NTLM authentication, therefore, if you disable it or use Kerberos authentication, both will prevent the attack.

4. Answer: c
Concept: **Cross-Site Scripting** (**XSS**) normally can be identified by using HTML tags and JavaScript. The target of the attack does not need any type of authentication. Cross site reverse forgery (XSRF or CSRF) needs the victim to be authenticated to the web server not the trusted server.

5. Answer: b
Concept: Passive reconnaissance is where information is gathered about the company, but no real action has been taken.

6. Answers: a, d, and f
Concept: Most IoT devices are used at home, however, the home user is not aware of any vulnerabilities. If we prevent them from connecting directly to the internet, change the default setting including the password, will make it safer as these passwords are freely available on the internet. You must not assume all IoT have printing capabilities as it uses the phrase printers and MFD devices. They connect to the internet via their network interface whether it is wireless or cabled.

7. Answer: e
Concept: We should never use weak passwords, however, if the exam says we are using them, then we need to accept it. The only way to mitigate the risk is to use a very short password expiry time.

8. Answer: c and e
Concept: A POODLE attack is a man in the middle that exploits a downgraded browser using SSL 3.0 with CBC.

9. Answer: e
Concept: A polymorphic virus mutates as it replicates; that is why the hash is changing.

10. Answer: c and d
Concept: Both salting and key stretching increase the password length by appending random characters to the end of the password.

11. Answer: c
Concept: DNSSEC encrypts DNS traffic preventing DNS poisoning and produces RRSIG records.

12. Answer: c
Concept: Pivoting is where an attacker enters your network via a vulnerable host then attacks a secondary host.

13. Answer: b
Concept: End-of-life systems are no longer supported, updated, or patched by the vendor, making them vulnerable to attack.

14. Answer: c
Concept: Regression testing is where a coding expert checks your code.

15. Answer: d
Concept: Loss of availability means the system is down; DoS is where one host takes down another and is the most likely answer.

16. Answer: a and c
Concept: Salting appends random characters to a password; therefore, it makes the password longer and more difficult to crack. If two people use the same password, the random characters appended to them make them unique.

17. Answer: d
Concept: If a system or a printer is vulnerable and it cannot be replaced, we can segment it from the rest of the network by placing it in a VLAN.

18 Answer: d
Concept: Sandboxing can be used to isolate an application for testing or patching or because it is dangerous. The Linux version is called chroot jail.

19. Answer: c
Concept: It takes someone with admin right to access all files, therefore the user would need to have privilege escalation to do so.

20. Answer: c
Concept: An email attack on a group of users is called spear phishing. Watch out in the exam for plural words. Phishing is attacking one person by email.

21. Answer: b
Concept: The attack method, first of all, uses a telephone, but the attacker has to leave a voicemail; this is known as vishing. For whaling to take place, the CEO would have to take some sort of action.

22. Answers: a, b, and c
Concept: A backdoor password is written by the application developer to be used at a later stage should the user lock themselves out. Another form is when you have to click several times to execute it.

23. Answers: b and d
Concept: Buffer overflow happens when an application receives more data than it can deal with. Both `strcpy` and `strcat` can collect strings of data that would cause a buffer overflow.

24. Answer: a
Concept: Input validation only accepts data in a certain format within a certain length and will prevent buffer overflow, integer overflow, and injection types attacks such as SQL injection.

25. Answer: b and c
Concept: Mantraps only allow one person in at a time and control who can access the facility; they are used frequently with data centers.

26. Answer: d
Concept: The UTM's first role is a firewall that prevents unauthorized access to the network. It can also provide URL and content filtering and malware protection.

27. Answer: c
Concept: A hacktivist is a politically motivated threat actor.

28. Answer: b
Concept: Banner grabbing is a technique that can interrogate the web servers; it can provide login details and patch level versions of a web server. Two common applications used for banner grabbing are netcat (nc) and telnet.

29. Answer: b
Concept: Dumpster diving is where an attacker will look for company information in the trash can. Most companies have a third party collect their paper waste and destroy it.

30. Answer: e
Concept: The frontend would be a web server and the backend would be a database such as a SQL server that would hold ticketing and credit card information.

31. Answer: a
Concept: Gray box penetration testing is where the tester has at least one piece of information.

32. Answer: d
Concept: In the Security+ exam, the phrase *1=1* means a SQL injection attack.

33. Answer: a
Concept: Penetration tests are intrusive and can cause damage, therefore, the type of scan would be an intrusive scan.

34. Answer: d and e
Concept: Social engineering authority gets an email from the CEO or the HR director, and urgency means that you have to deal with something immediately.

35. Answer: c
Concept: Files were created and transferred regularly, therefore, files being corrupted in transit looks the most likely—after all, the next file transfer worked.

36. Answer: b
Concept: If we did not change the default credentials for the firewall, this would explain why someone other than the administrators could access the firewall.

37. Answer: a
Concept: A black box penetration tester is given no information prior to starting the pen test.

38. Answer: c
Concept: SMIME is where a user will digitally sign an email to ensure integrity, and using their private key ensures non-repudiation of the message being sent.

39. Answer: a
Concept: Resource exhaustion is where a system has no resources left; the best example here is when the CPU is running at 100%, meaning full capacity.

40. Answer: c
Concept: When a monitoring system finds that attacks are in place and when a manual inspection does not find any, this is called a false positive.

41. Answer: c
Concept: When there are no users in the company, they will not be using the system.

42. Answer: c
Concept: Buffer overflow is where data larger than normal is being submitted; in this case, the normal number of bytes is 32, so 24,456 exceeds this and causes a buffer overflow.

43. Answers: b and c
Concept: The question asks for a message as a hoax; the only two items that produce messages are warning of monetary loss and claims of possible damage. All other items won't send a message.

44. Answer: c
Concept: A script kiddie does not have a high technical skill set, therefore, he has to use script or programs written by others; in this example, they are purchasing one from an illegal website.

45. Answer: e
Concept: A hacktivist is politically motivated.

46. Answer: d
Concept: An infected machine that is running as a bot member can be accessed 24/7, 365 days a year. If they were playing games, that traffic would be intermittent.

47. Answer: a
Concept: Arp is the only local attack, arp -s IP address MAC address, inserts static entries into the arp cache and prevents it from being poisoned.

48. Answer: d
Concept: Active reconnaissance is where an action is taken; this time, the attacker has got access to the system's registry.

49. Answer: c
Concept: Least privilege allows access and permissions to data.

50. Answer: d
Concept: Rolling out an image ensures that all of the computers have the same baseline, including security settings and patches.

Chapter 2: Technologies and Tools Practice Tests

Practice Test 5 – Solution

1. Because there is no allow rule for FTP or TCP port 21, explicit deny will be applied, preventing the download.

2. Port security disables the ports and reduces the functionality of the switch, however, 802.1x authenticates the device, so the ports remain open with rogue devices being prevented access.

3. Using IPSec between servers uses transport mode, but when IPSec is used over the internet, it uses tunnel mode.

4. A stateful firewall inspects incoming traffic down to the commands used and packet sizes and would realize that the three-way handshake is not being established and would prevent the SYN flood attack.

5. The role of the VPN concentrator is to set up the secure session for the VPN connection.

6. We would install a load balancer to deal with the vast amount of web traffic and we would set up affinity in the regions with limited bandwidth with all of the requests going to the same web server.

7. The best way to deal with a high volume of DDoS traffic is to use as a firewall to prevent this traffic entering your network.

8. DNS round robin can be used to balance web traffic as it rotates through the A records. The pitfall is that it does not know the status of the web server.

9. To capture commands going across the network, we need to use a packet sniffer, also known as a protocol analyzer.

10. A UDP port needs to be used for streaming video; TCP would be far too slow as it uses a three-way handshake.

11. To discover information such as the patch level version of a web server, we would use banner grabbing. Common tools for banner grabbing include telnet, nmap, or netcat (nc).

12. Nmap and NIDS can both identify when a new host enters your network.

13. A SIEM system should be implemented as it does real-time monitoring and can use an aggregation engine to identify attacks across the network.

14. To fulfill the policy, the security should store the security logs in a WORM drive (Write Once Read Many); this allows files to be copied to the drive but not altered or deleted.

15. Two tools that can identify an established session is the Windows command-line tool netstat and the Linux tool called netcat, also known as nc.

16. Security monitoring tools cannot analyze data if it is in an encrypted format.

17. A proxy filter has a URL filter to block access to certain websites, content filter to stop access to gaming websites, and web page caching to provide faster and more secure access to web pages. It cannot cache the stock exchange as the data is too volatile.

18. A reverse proxy authenticates incoming connections and decrypts incoming traffic so that the inline NIPS can monitor it.

19. A mobile telephone uses over-the-air updates where, ideally, the phone should have a full battery or be connected to a power socket.

20. A smartphone could be used to record a conversation and take videos and pictures of sensitive and private information.

21. To keep your business data separate from your personal data, you would storage segmentation, also known as containerization, to isolate the data from other data. This could be in the format of installing a micro SD card into the phone.

22. Using a **Virtual Desktop Infrastructure** (**VDI**) environment, the contractors would have an isolated desktop, depending on the network connections assigned to it. If they were to test applications, they could be sandboxed inside of their virtual machines.

23. Using a download manager would state how many connections are allowed and the amount of bandwidth that they are allowed to use.

24. You would first of all have to carry out carrier unlocking, known as jailbreaking, and then use a technique called sideloading to load the third-party software. This would not prevent you from using the Apple Store.

25. You would first of all have to carry out carrier unlocking, known as rooting, and then use a technique called sideloading to load the third-party software.

26. You would only remote wipe a mobile device if it was lost or stolen to prevent the data from falling into the wrong hands.

27. To diagnose the problems with a wireless access point, the network administrator would use a wireless packet sniffer to see the packets come from and to the wireless access point.

28. You can either use a wireless packet sniffer as the SSID is inside the packet destination for the wireless access point or an SSID de-cloak device to discover the disabled SSID.

29. GPS tagging inserts the location when a picture is taken.

30. A file integrity checker such as Microsoft's **System File Checker** (**SFC**) can determine whether the DLL files have been tampered with.

31. The administrator must first of all check the certificate to see whether it is still valid and then check whether it has been added to the Trusted Root Certification Authorities store on the local machine.

32. When the certificate was installed, it must have been valid and then added to the Trusted Root Certification Authorities store. The new employee must have deleted the local cache, removing the certificate from the Trusted Root Certification Authorities store.

33. When a laptop gets its internet connection via phone, this is known as tethering.

34. As most of the security has been circumvented without detection, it looks like a malicious insider threat has been carried out.

35. **Near Field Communication** (**NFC**) is a wireless payment system used by bank cards or mobile phones. It is limited to a distance of about 4 inches from the reader.

36. If the company has used more licenses than it originally purchased, this is called a license compliance violation and could result in a regulatory fine.

37. The all-in-one firewall device is called **Unified Threat Management** (**UTM**); this provides firewall, anti-malware, and anti-spam protection as well as content and URL filtering.

38. Once a remote user has been authenticated, if the security administrator implements **Network Access Control** (**NAC**), it would check that the device was fully patched before it was allowed onto the network.

39. If a company has an account lockout policy of three failed logins and they used a SIEM system, it would identify three failed logins, even if it was only one failed login on three separate machines. It also works in real time.

40. To prevent PII or sensitive information leaving the company by email, the administrator should implement a **Data Loss Prevention** (**DLP**) system. It uses a pattern match and if the information matches the pattern, it is prevented from leaving the network.

41. If the security administrator implemented **Data Execution Prevention** (**DEP**), any remote session would be limited to areas such as temporary internet files and not access the management of the system.

42. Downloading unauthorized software would reduce both the amount of available bandwidth and the amount of free disk space available.

43. A **Host-based Intrusion Prevention System** (**HIPS**) could be installed inside a virtual machine to prevent attacks.

44. An application whitelist lays out what application can be installed on a system. You can do this by adding the application name, the name of the `.msi` or `.exe` files or `.dll` binaries.

45. Storing information on a WORM drive prevents the deletion or amendment of the data stored there.

46. A security administrator would use a web application firewall to protect a web server's application and data from attack.

47. Push notification services inform a user that mail has arrived at their inbox.

48. ANT is a bespoke, low-power Bluetooth technology.

49. If the company implemented geofencing, it would prevent the high-end laptops from going outside of the boundaries set.

50. The biometric authentication failure acceptance rate allows the incorrect authentication method to gain access to a network.

Practice Test 6 – Solution

1. Router, firewall
2. Implicit deny
3. Tunnel, transport
4. Reverse proxy, inspect
5. Wireless packet sniffer, decloak
6. Secure tunnel
7. Port security, 802.1x
8. Honeypot
9. False positive
10. Input filters
11. Inline, passive
12. Banner Grabbing, packet sniffer
13. Nmap, telnet, and netcat
14. Netstat, netcat (nc)
15. SIEM, WORM
16. Site-to-site, always-on
17. Mail gateway, DLP
18. Nmap, NIDS
19. Signature-based, anomaly-based
20. Username, password, MAC
21. WPS, brute-force
22. Low-power directional
23. Load balancer, DNS round robin
24. Stateful
25. SIEM, correlation
26. Password age, **Time-Based One-Time Password (TOTP)**
27. HIPS
28. Remote wipe
29. DLP

30. Geofencing
31. Rooting/jailbreaking, sideloading
32. SSH
33. Whitelist
34. Context-aware authentication
35. UTM, malware filtering
36. DNSSEC, RRSIG
37. S/MIME, encryption
38. Off-boarding, exit interview
39. SRTP
40. Containerization, segmentation
41. Unauthorized software
42. LDAPS, 636
43. Group policy
44. Full disk encryption, screen locks
45. Valid, trusted root
46. Geofencing
47. DHCP snooping
48. FTPS
49. NAC
50. Shedding, pulp

Practice Test 7 – Solution

Description	Answer
Other than a firewall, what other device uses ACL?	Router
Setting up a non-secure remote session to your LAN.	Policy violation
IPSec mode between two servers on your LAN.	Transport mode
Add an application, EXE, or a DLL so it will run.	Whitelist
The system does not detect an attack.	False negative
What will you do if a mobile phone is lost or stolen?	Remote wipe
Prevent DNS poisoning by using DNSSEC. What records are created?	RRSIG
On a firewall, the result when the traffic is not on the allow rules.	Implicit deny
Lets you monitor the attack methods used.	Honeypot
Used to protect PII and sensitive information from leaving the company by email or USB.	DLP
A NIPS where all the traffic flows through it.	Inline

How to keep personal and business data separate on a cell phone.	Storage segmentation
A tool that tells you the patch version of a web server.	Banner grabbing
A firewall that can also perform malware inspection.	UTM
IPSec mode in a site-to-site VPN.	Tunnel mode
A passive device that works with a NIPS.	NIDS
A stolen Bluetooth phone used for texting your friends and family.	Bluejacking
A tool that can be used for banner grabbing.	Netcat (nc)
Can be used instead of a motion sensor to detect motion.	Camera
Adding a third-party application to your phone.	Sideloading
How to protect a mobile telephone.	FDE, screen locks
The system detects a virus but manual inspection contradicts it.	False positive
Secure remote access protocol that can use a GUI to access a router.	SSH
How you could block unwanted applications.	Blacklist
Used for secure transfer of data between two hosts.	TLS

Practice Test 8 – Mock Exam 2 – Solution

1. Answer: c
Concept: When there is no allow rule in either a firewall or router, the incoming traffic gets the last rule, which is deny all. This is known as implicit deny.

2. Answer: e
Concept: Enabling port security on the switch blocks all connections to the wall jack as the port is turned off.

3. Answer: b
Concept: **Network Access Control** (**NAC**) checks that clients are patched, and this occurs after the authentication process. A non-compliant machine that is unpatched is placed in a quarantine or boundary network where the required updates are obtained from a remediation server. In this case, there is no way to obtain updates. Therefore, once the client has been authenticated, there will be a host health check and if the client is not patched, the connection will drop.

4. Answer: b
Concept: When additional switches are added to the network, you must ensure that there is loop protection by using the spanning tree protocol. If this is not done, then there will be broadcasting between switches, known as looping, which will slow the traffic down. Spanning tree will have some ports forward, block or listen for traffic to prevent looping.

5. Answer: c
Concept: **Near Field Communication** (**NFC**) is a contactless payment method over a distance of 4 inches or 10 centimeters.

6. Answer: d
Concept: The purpose of the VPN concentrator is to create the secure sessions for VPN connections.

7. Answer: b and c
Concept: `netstat -an` is a Microsoft product that will show connections and netcat, normally known as nc, shows established connection as it is a Unix open source utility.

8. Answer: c
Concept: If you put your voice traffic, also known as videoconferencing, into its own VLAN, it is separated from the rest of the network and bandwidth will be guaranteed. This will result in better quality videoconferencing.

9. Answer: a
Concept: POP3 is a legacy version of email that does not keep a copy on the server. Upgrading will allow the mail administrator to backup the emails that remain on the mail server.

10. Answer: c
Concept: When setting IPSec between hosts on the internal LAN, IPSec transport mode should be used where only the ESP is encrypted. When using IPSec in a VPN as L2TP/IPSec, it should be used in tunnel mode where both the AH and ESP are encrypted.

11. Answers: b, c, d, e, f, and g
Concept: Proxy server can perform web page caching, URL and content filtering. The UTM can perform malware inspection and URL and content filtering.

12. Answer: d
Concept: The whitelist is a list of allowed applications, EXE files, and DLL binaries. Since the only exception was `payroll.dll`, we need to add the DLL binary to the whitelist.

13. Answer: b
Concept: An inline NIPS inspects all traffic flowing through it, however, an encrypted packet cannot be inspected by any security device in the Security+ exam.

14. Answer: c
Concept: TLS is used in the Security+ exam for the encryption of mail between mail servers. The encryption of mail between two people uses PGP.

15. Answer: b
Concept: Geolocation shows you the location where the equipment is. Another option would be to use geofencing—that would alert the security administrator when each piece of equipment left the theatre.

16. Answer: c
Concept: **False Acceptance Rate (FAR)** is where a person who should not have access to a system gains access because of a biometric authentication error.

17. Answer: b
Concept: A HIPS is a host-based intrusion prevention system that can help to prevent attacks.

18. Answer: c and e
Concept: A site-to-site VPN can be used to connect two sites together and it needs to use always-on mode as it is a permanent connection.

19. Answer: b and d
Concept: Nmap is a tool that can map out the whole network showing hosts and detailed information about them. NIDS can alert you when a computer has just joined the network as it uses sensors and collectors to do so.

20. Answer: e
Concept: The CER is where the FAR and FRR are both equal. The lower the CER, the better the biometric system as there are fewer errors.

21. Answer: d
Concept: A WORM drive is write once read many, this means that data cannot be deleted, altered, or tampered with so that the log files can be protected.

22. Answer: d
Concept: The best ways to dispose of a hard drive from best to worst are shred, pulverize, and degauss.

23. Answer: c, e
Concept: In the Security+ exam, when you see names in clear text and a hash value, this is a hash of the password. The preceding is the MD5 hash of the word `password`, one of the most common passwords. This is the output from a password cracker.

24. Answer: c
Concept: In the Security+ exam, the fastest backup is the snapshot. It should really be the fastest restore. Snapshots are normally a rollback option.

25. Answer: b and e
Concept: A hardened operating system has no vulnerabilities. The SIEM system is giving the wrong information; this is known as a false positive. SIEM systems measure different types of packets using a separate input filter for each, and using the incorrect filter will produce false positives.

26. Answer: c
Concept: Context-aware authentication can be set up so that the devices only operate in the UK and if someone tried to use them in another country, the device would be disabled.

27. Answer: c
Concept: DNS round robin is a technique where the web requests are rotated through each DNS record for web servers balancing the incoming requests.

28. Answer: b
Concept: The best ways of destroying paper data, from best to worst, are burning, pulping, then shredding.

29. Answer: c
Concept: The company has a license compliance violation as all software is licensed and using more copies of software than the licenses that you purchase is breaking the law.

30. Answer: c
Concept: A honeypot is a website made to look like a legitimate website with lowered security so that security teams can monitor the attack methods being used, then they can mitigate the risk. A number of honeypots is called a honeynet.

31. Answer: b and c
Concept: When the SSID is disabled, the SSID can be attached to the packet header. Both a SSID decloak device and a wireless scanner/wireless packet sniffer can capture the SSID from the packet.

32. Answer: a
Concept: The fastest physical backup is a full backup as each physical backup starts with a full backup.

33. Answer: c
Concept: Voice traffic operates on a protocol called Real Time Protocol and the secure version is **Secure Real-Time Protocol (SRTP)**.

34. Answer: b, c, and g
Concept: The cell phones will need screen locks, so they log out; they will need strong password to prevent them from being guessed and device encryption to encrypt the data at rest.

35. Answer: d
Concept: Secure traffic between two mail servers and data in transit is TLS. S/MIME and PGP are used between two people.

36. Answer: c
Concept: Split tunneling is where someone first launches a secure session to their company's LAN and then makes another session that is unsecure. The attacker then gains access to the company's network via the unsecure session.

37. Answer: d
Concept: **Network Access Control** (**NAC**) kicks in after a remote connection has been made to ensure that the device is fully patched and has no virus, making the machine compliant. A non-compliant machine is placed in a quarantined network, where the remediation server gives them access to missing patched; they will then gain access to the network.

38. Answer: d
Concept: A wireless scanner can capture packets from and to the wireless access point, so that they can troubleshoot where the problem is arising. They will also be able to see rejected packets.

39. Answer: d
Concept: A thin wireless controller pushes out new configuration files to all wireless access points from a central location.

40. Answer: b and c
Concept: To install a firewall, it must be powered on. The only rule in the firewall (or router) is deny all. Therefore, the default setting is *block all*, allow by exception, where you would configure allow rules.

41. Answer: c
Concept: A credentialed scan is a passive scan that can provide the details of the server as well as missing patches. A non-credentialed scan is also passive but can only identify missing patches.

42. Answer: d
Concept: **Data Loss Prevention** (**DLP**) prevents PII or sensitive information from leaving the company by blocking data that matches the pattern. It can block emails and prevent data being put on external drives.

43. Answer: c
Concept: Both Kerberos and a SIEM system are time-dependent and need to maintain accurate time by synchronizing with the atomic clock or any reference time clock.

44. Answer: d
Concept: A reverse proxy authenticates incoming connections and has the ability to decrypt incoming data.

45. Answer: b and c
Concept: Tethering his mobile phone to the laptop will provide a much more secure internet connection. Using a L2TP/IPSEC VPN provides the most secure session to the credit card portal.

46. Answer: d
Concept: A load balancer knows the status of each web server, therefore, it passes requests to the least utilized host.

47. Answer: b and d
Concept: Although better security can be provided by using multifactor authentication, the most common method is the single factor username and password.

48. Answer: b and e
Concept: Unlocking an iOS phone is called jailbreaking; routing is when it is an Android phone. Loading unauthorized third-party apps is called sideloading.

49. Answer: b
Concept: We do not wish DDoS traffic to enter our network. There, we will install a stateful firewall as it will inspect the incoming traffic and deny the DDoS traffic access to the network. We want to prevent the DDoS traffic from arriving.

50. Answer: c and e
Concept: A L2TP/IPSec is externally set up in tunnel mode, whereas, server to server with a LAN is transport mode. The only three protocols used with L2TP/IPSec are DES, 3DES, and AES. AES can operate up to 256 bits, this makes it the most secure.

Chapter 3: Architecture and Design Practice Tests

Practice Test 9 – Solution

1. Prior to creating policies, companies should look at all regulations and frameworks to ensure that they comply with them.

2. COBIT and ITIL are non-regulatory and not legally enforceable as they are both good practice frameworks.

3. Purchasing broadband from two different companies provides vendor diversity, therefore, if one company fails, then the other still provides broadband.

4. The boundary layer between the LAN and the WAN is called the DMZ; it hosts the extranet web server that is normally used for suppliers and needs credentials to access it.

5. If a laptop had sensitive information such as research and development data, the IT team could isolate it from the network by air gapping it so nobody could connect to it.

6. When full disk encryption such as BitLocker is used on a laptop, the laptop needs to have either a TPM chip or an HSM to store the encryption keys.

7. An IT security team would roll out a honeypot when they want to observe the attack methods being used by an attacker. The benefits would be to enable them to defend against such an attack.

8. A network administrator would use a load balancer to balance the website traffic so that each request would go to the least utilized host, but would use a firewall to prevent the DDoS traffic from entering the company network.

9. A site-to-site VPN is a solution that can connect two different locations as long as it is set to always on; this is a much cheaper solution that a leased line.

10. Port mirroring or a tap can capture traffic going to a port on a switch and display it on another device for analysis.

11. The role of the VPN concentrator is to set up a secure session.

12. If I am using full disk encryption, the trust model being used is known as a hardware root of trust.

13. Standard operating procedures are the step-by-step instructions on how to carry out a task.

14. The company would set this laptop up so that it is air gapped—that would isolate it from the network.

15. You would create four VLANs and put each company in its own VLAN, therefore, isolating them from each other. This would give control to each VLAN and reduce the broadcast domains.

16. If an application will not run or install, it is simply because it has not been added to the whitelist; it does not necessarily need to be on the blacklist. The blacklist is for applications that will never be installed as they are banned.

17. The most common threat to printers and multifunction devices would be the network interface as most devices are now fully connected.

18. Sandboxing is where an isolated virtual machine can be used for patching, testing, or isolation of a dangerous application, therefore, the research and development department would put it in a sandbox.

19. The temperature rise is due to the additional increase in computers but it looks like they have not set up the hot aisles and cold aisles to regulate the temperature.

20. The professor has failed to change the default username or the default password of each of these devices, leaving himself vulnerable to attack.

21. A refrigerator comes under the category of IoT and the defibrillator comes under the category SoC.

22. Errors that are customer-facing should be bland, giving away very little information, whereas the errors for the IT team should be as long and detailed as possible. Errors should not cause a system to stop.

23. Both the black box and white box penetration testers use fuzzing, a technique that puts random information into an application to see what random output it provides. The white box tester is doing this with newly developed applications so that they are secure before moving into production.

24. The first technique to mask data would be obfuscation as it obscures the data; the second technique for embedding data would be steganography as it hides data inside other data.

25. The best method for preventing a SQL injection attack would be to use a stored procedure where a sealed script is created and run by using the script name. The secondary way to prevent SQL injection would be input validation where the input is controlled.

26. A zero-day virus cannot be detected by any monitoring system or antivirus solution; it can only be detected by using a baseline where an earlier baseline is compared to the current baseline.

27. The benefit of using a machine template or an imaging package such as a ghost to image a computer is that it produces a consistent baseline.

28. An immutable system is where the complete components are replaced rather than updated, therefore, it would never be patched as it would be fully replaced.

29. The only cloud model that allows you to host bespoke systems in the cloud and maintain them is **Platform as a service** (**PaaS**). An example would be Azure.

30. Software as a service is where a vendor writes an application and then leases it but customization is forbidden. Examples would be Spotify or Office 365.

31. Type I hypervisors are bare metal and require no operating system, whereas a Type II hypervisor sits on top of an operating system, for example, Oracle's VirtualBox.

32. If the US Army decided to move all of their systems to the cloud, they would adopt a private cloud where they would own the whole environment and be isolated from everyone else due to security.

33. If an IT training company needed an environment for a word-processing course, they would lease little resources from the cloud provider but if they required a Skype or SharePoint environment, they could lease high-end servers—all they have to do is to send the image to the cloud provider, who would roll it out.

34. The company needs to put version control on each document and have a master list on the intranet as to what is the latest version. That way, older versions could be destroyed.

35. The staging phase in SDLC is where the application is tested with production data.

36. Waterfall is where one stage must be completed fully before the next stage commences. Agile can start all phases at the same time; its main aim is customer satisfaction. It is very similar to scrum.

37. A camera is a physical device that can capture both pictures and video, therefore, capturing motion and providing non-repudiation as the person is captured on film.

38. A Faraday cage can be built over a WLAN, preventing emissions from escaping and blocking incoming wireless communications.

39. The company is adopting key management where they ensure that all keys are accounted for and do not leave the premises so keys cannot be cut.

40. Protected distribution or conduits can be used to house cabling and prevent them from being attacked by rodents.

41. VM escape is where an attacker launches an attack from a vulnerable virtual machine and attacks the host housing all of the virtual machines.

42. VM sprawl is where an unmanaged virtual machine has been added to your virtual network, as it is not known, it will not be regularly patched and will become vulnerable to attack.

43. A NAT hides the internal network and protects it from attack by a third party.

44. DNSSEC can be used to encrypt all DNS traffic and prevent DNS poisoning and it produces RRSIG records.

45. DHCP snooping can prevent IP addresses from rogue access points from operating in your network. It prevents those addresses from being offered to client computers.

46. The company owns the equipment in a CYOD environment, therefore, when someone leaves the company, there can be no argument over who owns the data, whereas, in a BYOD environment, problems relating to data ownership could arise.

47. **Near Field Communication** (**NFC**) is used for contactless card payments.

48. I could insert an SD card or similar card to keep my business data separate from my personal data; this is known as containerization or storage segmentation.

49. When a network load balancer is set to affinity, it sends the client request to the same web server and does not balance it across all of the hosts.

50. If I don't have a load balancer, I can use DNS round robin to rotate the incoming requests to each web server by going to each of the DNS records in turn.

Practice Test 10 – Solution

1. VLAN, airgaps
2. DMZ, WAN, extranet
3. Sprawl
4. Store procedures, input
5. NAT, PAT
6. Dead
7. Sensors, collectors
8. Aggregation
9. Software, modified
10. Escape
11. SIEM, correlation
12. Site-to-site, always on

13. False, input
14. Community cloud
15. Cloud access security broker
16. Refinery, SCADA
17. VM sprawl
18. Obfuscation, steganography
19. Private cloud, infrastructure, configure
20. Mantraps, HVAC, overheating

21. Shoulder, screen filters
22. Staging, data, sandboxing
23. Image, baseline
24. Industry frameworks, credit card
25. Load balancer, DDoS mitigator, firewall
26. White, fuzzing, code, vulnerabilities
27. Code
28. TPM
29. Control diversity
30. Regulatory framework
31. Tethering
32. Honeypot
33. Defence in depth, next
34. Storage segmentation, containerization
35. Non-persistent, snapshot
36. Web of trust, hardware root of trust, CAs, trust model
37. Cannot
38. Single, one, double, two, 6
39. Strong, screen locks, encryption
40. Guides
41. Platform
42. IoT, SoC
43. Waterfall, agile
44. Real time, SRTP
45. Security, SAML
46. Positive, hardened, wrong
47. Time synchronization
48. Username and passwords, immediately, directly
49. Port mirror, tap
50. Isolated, storage segmentation

Practice Test 11 – Solution

Description	Answer
A boundary layer between the LAN and the WAN.	DMZ
Taking a list of applications on a laptop 2 months apart.	Baseline
Prevents a SQL injection attack.	Stored procedure
A control that helps you rekey an ID badge.	Administrative
Testing an application with real data prior to going into production.	Staging
Attack a virtual host from a guest virtual machine.	VM escape
Type of switch that connects multiple switches together.	Aggregation
Used to isolate applications for patching, isolation, or testing.	Sandboxing
Wireless network for visitors or employees at lunchtime.	Guest
The attack vector for visitors or employees.	Network interface
A life support machine is an example of this.	SoC
Leasing a software package on the cloud.	SaaS
A control that mitigates risk.	Technical
Putting an unmanaged VM onto a virtual network.	VM sprawl
To prevent an attack on a home IoT device, turn off the…	Internet connection
Allows you to filter off traffic for analysis.	Tap or port mirror
A cloud model that gives you more control.	Private cloud
A contained environment that's used to secure contractors' desktops.	VDI
Isolation of a machine from the local network.	Air gap
Deploying your application into the cloud.	PaaS
Cloud model where companies share the cost of resources.	Community cloud
A configuration that you can roll back.	Non-persistent
A cloud service that gives you more control.	IaaS
A web server located in the DMZ.	Extranet
Regulates temperature using hot and cold aisles.	HVAC

Practice Test 12 – Mock Exam 3 – Solution

1. Answer: d
Concept: When a computer or device is air gapped, it is not connected to the network.

2. Answer: b
Concept: A baseline is a list of installed applications, updates, and settings. If a baseline had been used, everyone would have the same settings.

3. Answer: b
Concept: A honeypot allows the security administrator to attract potential attackers and monitor the attack method being utilized.

4. Answer: c, e, and g
Concept: Screen savers should be implemented to ensure that when a phone is idle, it is logged out. Strong passwords, also known as complex passwords, should be used to secure access to the phone. FDE should also be used to encrypt the data at rest to protect it.

5. Answer: b
Concept: Infrastructure as a service is where you install, configure, and patch the operating system, therefore having more control over how it is set up and configured.

6. Answer: c and e
Concept: When you use additional storage on a device such as an SD card, this is known as containerization or storage segmentation. Also, an isolated guest virtual machine is known as containers.

7. Answer: c
Concept: Both the tablet and life support systems use integrated circuits known as chips. Apple watches, smartphones, and computer motherboards come under this category known as **system on a chip** (**SoC**).

8. Answer: b
Concept: VDI is a virtual desktop infrastructure where a pool of virtual desktops is created and each person has their own desktop that is accessed only by them. Note, the question did not say these workers were remote, therefore the VPN was ruled out.

9. Answer: d
Concept: Both RAID 5 and 6 can use four disks, however, RAID 5 has single parity and can only lose one disk. RAID 6 has dual parity and can lose two disks, making it more resilient. RAID 10 provides better redundancy than RAID 6.

10. Answer: a
Concept: Most MFD devices have a network interface enabling them to be accessed by everyone on the network. The network interface could be used by a remote attacker.

11. Answer: d
Concept: VM sprawl is where an unmanaged virtual machine is placed on your virtual network. Because the administrator does not know about its existence, it is never patched, making it vulnerable.

12. Answer: d
Concept: A Faraday cage acts as a force field to prevent electrical current and wireless emissions from coming into or leaving a network. The Faraday cage prevents electromagnetic radiation emanating from electronic equipment.

13. Answer: b, e, and f
Concept: All errors should be logged and the application must keep running. On the user side, the errors should be small and generic so an attacker has very little detail. On the system administrator side, the error should be long and very detailed so he can investigate it.

14. Answer: a
Concept: Agile and scrum are very similar where they can incrementally start different phases of the SDLC to provide faster delivery and customer satisfaction.

15. Answer: c
Concept: CSP can increase or decrease cloud resources at the drop of a hat. Therefore, as a new company increases its sales and number of employees, the CSP can provide them with the resources they need.

16. Answer: a
Concept: A private cloud is known as a single tenant where you have total control of the environment.

17. Answer: a
Concepts: Regulatory framework standards are legally enforceable whereas user guides are not. If we exceed the regulatory standards, we can prove to a court that we are very responsible and compliant with current regulations.

18. Answer: c
Concept: An intranet website sits on your LAN and has company sensitive data. An extranet is located in the DMZ, a boundary layer, and is accessed by username and password. This would be used to share information with distributors or suppliers.

19. Answer: d
Concept: A SIEM system is a real-time monitoring system that has a correlation engine. In this example, the attacker is attempting to only log in once to each machine, so he does not get locked out and records events in the security log. If a SIEM system provides a false positive, it will be due to using the wrong input filter.

20. Answer: d
Concept: Whitelists are used to control what software can be installed, therefore, if it is not on the whitelist, you can never install it. Blacklists are used to control banned applications.

21. Answer: a
Concept: A conduit is used to house and protect the cables that he is laying.

22. Answer: d
Concept: Non-persistent configuration allows you to roll back to a previous state and an example of this could be a snapshot of a virtual machine.

23. Answer: d
Concept: A community cloud is where people in the same industry share the cost and running of a cloud application. For example, a group of lawyers are not happy with the retail software so they contribute to have a cloud provider create a bespoke application that they all use.

24. Answer: a
Concept: A port mirror captures the traffic in and out of a port and stores it on another device. Sometimes this is known as a tap.

25. Answer: d
Concept: Placing any device into a VLAN separates it from the rest of the network. The administrator realized the legacy devices were vulnerable to attack as no updates were available.

26. Answer: d
Concept: An image can be created with least functionality and all of the latest security updates installed. This way, the security team knows what the security baseline of each computer is.

27. Answer: b
Concept: When attacks are being made, the first step is usually identifying the source of the attack, however, if it is a rapidly spreading virus, it is an exception and it must be quarantined, isolated, or contained to stop it spreading.

28. Answer: d
Concept: Data centers will normally have a HVAC system that consists of hot and cold aisles that regulate the air temperature by cold airflow inward and the hot airflow outward.

29. Answer: b
Concept: Although many of the selections could be implemented, the best method for securing the laptops is to introduce least functionality in this method—only the essentials applications and services are available.

30. Answer: d
Concept: Platform as a service is a cloud environment where applications can be developed. SaaS is bespoke software provided with the cloud provider and cannot be modified.

31. Answer: d
Concept: VM escape is where a guest machine is exploited so that the host can be attacked, taking down the virtual host. Pivoting is where an attacker (in a physical environment) gains access via a vulnerable computer to attack a computer on the network.

32. Answer: a
Concept: Cable locks can lock either laptops or tablets to a desktop to prevent theft. If you visit a store selling tablets, all of these tablets have cable locks so that the tablet can be picked up but not stolen.

33. Answer: d
Concept: Stored procedures are sealed SQL scripts and the BEST way to prevent SQL injection attacks. Another way is to use input validation.

34. Answer: a
Concept: A public cloud is when a CSP will host many different companies on the same hardware.

35. Answer: c
Concept: Staging is the process of testing an application with production data. SDLC is development—where an application is created. Testing—they test the functionality. Staging—test with production data. Production—it is rolled out.

36. Answer: d
Concept: When too much data is inserted into a data field, this is known as a buffer overflow attack.

37. Answer: a
Concept: An immutable system is where components are replaced rather than repaired.

38. Answer: a and e
Concept: A guest hotspot would allow visitors to access the internet. Employees may not have internet access when at work due to their personal devices being prohibited, therefore, they could use the guest Wi-Fi at lunchtime.

39. Answer: c
Concept: The only way to identify when a person's access level increases is by continuous monitoring. With permission auditing and review, you might only audit every 3 or 6 months and this is not immediate.

40. Answer: b
Concept: Obfuscation obscures source code so that it cannot be read by a third party. **Expression OR (XOR)** can swap values of distinct variables, making them obscure.

41. Answer: d
Concept: Sandboxing is an isolated virtual machine that can be used to test, patch, or isolate an application or operating system.

42. Answer: a
Concept: A site-to-site VPN in "always-on" mode is a permanent connection between two sites. It is much cheaper than purchasing a lease line or running a fiber cable.

43. Answer: b
Concept: The CEO has used an administrative control and the systems administrator has then implemented technical controls. As two controls were used, this should be deemed control diversity.

44. Answer: b
Concept: A camera can take pictures and capture video. They can be used in evidence in case of an investigation.

45. Answer: a, b
Concept: SCADA systems are used to control and monitor plant and equipment on an industrial basis. They have a control room with different stages of production.

46. Answer: b
Concept: BitLocker is an example of FDE and needs either a TPM chip or HSM to install the keys.

47. Answer: b, d
Concept: Guards check the identity of those people entering the data center. A mantrap ensures that only one person accesses the data center at a time and can be controlled by the guard.

48. Answer: b
Concept: When evidence is collected, they take the regional time known as the record time offset. They can use time normalization by converting it into the same time zone, such as GMT, to establish how data is moved between the criminals.

49. Answer: c
Concept: Waterfall is one of the oldest SDLC methodologies, where one stage of the project is finished before moving onto the next stage.

50. Answer: d
Concept: There are only two ways to isolate the mail server: put it in a VLAN or a DMZ. Air gapping it would mean that nobody could access any email.

Chapter 4: Identity and Access Management Practice Tests

Practice Test 13 – Solution

1. **Mandatory Access Control** (**MAC**) is based on the classification of the data. The creator of the data, also known as the owner, is responsible for its classification.

2. The Microsoft authentication method that uses tickets is called Kerberos; it uses updated sequence numbers and timestamps. It can prevent pass the hash and replay attacks.

3. The first stage is identification is where a username or smart card is used, followed by authentication where a password or pin is inserted and then the authorization stage where your access to resources is determined.

4. The three main components of an AAA solution are Authentication, Authorization, and Accounting.

5. The UDP-based AAA solution is RADIUS. The two that are TCP-based are TACACS+ and DIAMETER.

6. The directory services protocol that stores object in an X500 format is **Lightweight Directory Access Protocol** (**LDAP**).

7. Rule-based authentication can be used for the whole company or department. For example, contractors are allowed access from 9 a.m. to 5 p.m.

8. Role-based authentication is used for a subset of a department completing a subset of duties. For example, two people in finance control the petty cash.

9. Someone who works in finished goods only needs a standard user account for work purposes.

10. A shared account makes it impossible to audit or log to an individual user as several people could use this account.

11. **False Acceptance Rate (FAR)**, used in biometrics, will incorrectly accept an access attempt by unauthorized users.

12. The password is the most common authentication factor that is inserted incorrectly inserted; however, it is rejected by the system.

13. The identity portion of access management is where either a username or smart card is inserted to identify the person.

14. The authorization phase follows identification and authentication; this is where a user's access is determined.

15. The authentication phase is where a password or pin is inserted.

16. RADIUS and TACACS+ are both server use accounting to track when users access and leave a system.

17. Federation services use cookies to authenticate users.

18. The protocol being used is OAuth2.0 but the authentication type is known as OpenID Connect.

19. Biometric authentication uses the crossover error rate to measure when the Failure Acceptance Rate is equal to the **Failure Rejection Rate (FRR)**.

20. Group policy can be used to prevent someone from using a CD/DVD drives as well as setting up the password policy for the whole domain.

21. Federation services is a third party to third party authentication model that uses extended attributes.

22. Open source federation services are called Shibboleth.

23. Federation services through a WAP are called RADIUS federation.

24. NTLM authentication can be subjected to a pass the hash attack. The best way to prevent it to use Kerberos and the other way is to disable NTLM.

25. Using **Single Sign-On (SSO)** allows you to access the systems using one set of credentials.

26. Your gait is the way you walk, therefore it comes under the something you do authentication model.

27. You should know the birth date, therefore, it comes under the something you know authentication model.

28. A natural signature comes under the something you do authentication model.

29. A password, pin, and birth date are all something that you know, therefore, they are a single factor.

30. An iris, retina, fingerprint, and palm are all parts of the body that come under the something you have authentication model; therefore, they are a single factor.

31. A password is something that you know and a token fob is something you have; therefore, they are two factors.

32. A password is something that you know while a token fob and TOTP comes via a handheld device and is something you have; therefore, they are two factors.

33. A security guard is a deterrent who checks identity but is also a biometric scanner as they can carry out facial recognition.

34. Failure Acceptance Rate will allow someone not authorized to access the systems.

35. Kerberos replaced NTLM; it is more secure as the credentials are stored in an Active Directory database, and prevents a pass the hash attack.

36. CHAP authentication has the authenticator send the challenge that is to encrypt the login password.

37. PAP is an authentication protocol where the password is sent in clear text.

38. Kerberos is a Microsoft authentication protocol that provides mutual authentication and single sign-on and is time-dependent. Each computer must be within 5 minutes of the domain controller's time.

39. Context-aware authentication can be used for location-based authentication.

40. **Security Assertion Markup Language (SAML)** is XML-based and used with federation services.

41. Federation services are used between third parties and extended attributes are used to form a claim. Extended attributes are unique to a user, for example, their employee ID or email address with a password.

42. RADIUS federation is federated services where the connection method is using wireless technology.

43. Biometric faults are measured by looking at the FAR and the FRR. On a graph, the CER is where they cross over as they are equal. A low CER indicates more reliability.

44. An auditor needs to be able to audit or monitor so that they can identify the individual who is responsible. Using shared accounts prohibits them from doing this.

45. Voice recognition technology is normally based on an American- or English-based voice, therefore, for it to be successful for a Scottish dialect it would have to be updated to accept a Scottish regional accent.

46. Administrator and service technicians would need privileged accounts to give them the privileges to perform their jobs.

47. The CAC card is a smart card used extensively by military personnel; in addition to being a smart card, it also has the blood group and which part of the military they belong to, for example, Army, Navy, or Air Force.

48. You will need the old private key associated with the old public key that was used to encrypt the data in the first place.

49. The most simplified way to set up accounts in an Active Directory environment when smart cards are not an option is to use usernames and passwords.

50. The IT team should disable the account and reset the password and take possession of company-owned computer equipment. The HR team should be responsible for performing an exit interview to discover why they are leaving.

Practice Test 14 – Solution

1. User
2. Mandatory Access Control
3. Privileged
4. Know
5. Accounting
6. Discretionary Access Control
7. PAP

8. Wireless, certificate
9. Somewhere
10. Context-aware
11. Federation, SAML
12. Smart card
13. Kerberos, time
14. Authorization
15. RADIUS, TACACS+, DIAMETER
16. OAuth, OpenID Connect
17. CHAP, hash
18. Single sign-on
19. LDAP, LDAPS

20. Attribute-based access control
21. Do
22. Role-based access control
23. Identification, smart, username
24. Proximity card
25. Smart card
26. Physical
27. False Rejection Rate
28. Crossover Error Rate
29. TOTP, HOTP
30. Shared accounts
31. Time and day restrictions
32. False Acceptance Rate
33. Exit interviews, off-boarding
34. Standard naming convention
35. Password complexity
36. Permissions auditing
37. Shibboleth
38. Password history, account lockout
39. Least privilege
40. Credential management
41. Increase
42. Service account
43. Smart card, CAC
44. Group policy
45. Rule-based Access Control
46. Kerberos, disabling
47. Username, password

48. Account expiry
49. Owner, custodian, administrator
50. Shared secret

Practice Test 15 – Solution

Description	Answer
What uses port 1813?	RADIUS accounting
What comes after identification during access management?	Authentication
Two policies that affect BYOD.	AUP, on-boarding
Something you do.	Signature, gait
Differentiate between different items in a report.	Standard naming convention
What uses TCP port 49?	TACACS+
Control access for a whole department.	Rule-based access control
Two accounts that have higher than user privilege.	Privileged, service
What type of device is an iris scanner?	Physical
What type of authentication is company A and company B?	Federation
Prevents a single user from accessing the system once they have finished work.	Time-of-day restriction
This is done prior to leaving a company.	Exit interview
Something you know.	Password and PIN
Where password policies are set up.	Group policy
A password with a 30-60 second time limit.	TOTP
What is third-party to third-party authentication using extended attributes that connect using a wireless connection?	RADIUS federation
Controls access for a subset of duties and a subset of a department.	Role-based access control
Lets you authenticate using your Facebook account and its protocol.	OpenID Connect, OAuth
Access management based on file classification; for example, a secret.	MAC
Who gives access to classified data?	Administrator
Something you have.	Token fob, read proximity card

Who stores classified data?	Custodian
Who is the person who decides the classification of a document?	Owner
Located-based authentication.	Context-aware
Access based on department or location.	ABAC

Practice Test 16 – Mock Exam 4 – Solution

1. Answer: a
Concept: VPN and 802.1x authenticated switches can both be RADIUS clients. To connect to a RADIUS server, a shared secret (sometimes called a Shared Key in the Security+ exam) is required.

2. Answer: b, d, e, f, and g
Concept: A natural signature and handwriting are both basically the same. Tap a screen or swiping a card are also something you do. Your gait is how you walk.

3. Answer: d
Concept: The attacker has tried different formats of username and password using common standard naming conventions. After this is established, he then tries to guess the password.

4. Answer: f
Concept: Authentication between two third parties is federation services, but when the connection method is wireless, it is then RADIUS federation.

5. Answer: b
Concept: When a classified document is being written, it is the data owner (writer) who decides on the classification in the first place. They are the best entity to consult to see whether the document needs downgrading. In the Security+ exam, the custodian stores and manages the data and the administrator gives access to the data.

6. Answer: c
Concept: **Crossover Error Rate (CER)** is where the **False Rejection Rate (FRR)** is equal to the **False Acceptance Rate (FAR)**. A low-value CER is the mark of a good biometric access control system.

7. Answer: d
Concept: Shibboleth is an open source federation service that uses cookies.

8. Answer: c and d
Concept: As they are temporary workers, we will use account expiry to ensure that they cannot access the systems once their contract expires. Time and day restrictions are set up on an individual basis so that they don't have access when they are off the clock.

9. Answer: b and c
Concepts: If shared accounts are being used, it is impossible to audit or monitor a single employee.

10. Answer: d
Concept: **HMAC-based One-Time Password** (HOTP) does not expire over a period of time. It expires on first use. TOTP expires 30-60 seconds after issue.

11. Answer: c
Concept: **Discretionary Access Control** (DAC) can be used with either users or groups. Therefore, it can be user-based, sometimes known as user-centric.

12. Answer: b
Concept: In this case, the bank uses a One-Time Password, which is time-sensitive and will expire after a short period of time. Once the code is entered, it can never be reused.

13. Answer: b
Concept: Username, password, and PIN are something that you know and a smart card is something you have and then add a PIN therefore, it is single factor but multifactor factor when the smart card is used.

14. Answer: a
Concept: If the company had logged and reviewed the usage, they would have noticed the trend of the famous people's account being accessed by a single user.

15. Answer: c
Concept: Brute force uses every available combination and will eventually crack the password. The longer the password, the more compute resources it will take to crack it. The only way to prevent a brute force attack is to have an account lockout with a low value.

16. Answer: b
Concept: False Acceptance Rate is where the biometric will incorrectly accept an access attempt by an unauthorized user.

17. Answer: c and d
Concept: SAML is an XML-based open standard that allows service providers to exchange authentication information with identity providers. OTP uses SOAP credentials via WSS and SMS. SOAP is an XML-based protocol.

18. Answer: a
Concept: DIAMETER is an upgrade to the RADIUS server that uses EAP.

19. Answer: b
Concept: A privileged account has admin rights, used to complete admin tasks. A service account is used to run a particular service such as an antivirus on a computer.

20. Answer: b
Concept: OAuth uses tokens and can be used with OpenID Connect, using your Facebook account to authenticate you.

21. Answer: d
Concept: A token is a physical device you have.

22. Answer: d
Concept: **Attribute-Based Access Control** (**ABAC**) would be used in this instance by giving control based on the office location in their directory service account.

23. Answer: d
Concept: Context-aware authentication looks to see the location of the person requesting the information.

24. Answer: b, c, e, and f
Concept: If the company is using group-based access control, then the solution will also be group-based. Each intern needs an individual account, so that they are accountable for their actions. If we then create a group called interns and give it read access to the data, we then just need to add the individual accounts to the group.

25. Answer: c
Concept: The dispatch workers are only doing minor tasks in the computer systems, therefore, they only require user permissions.

26. Answer: e
Concept: Role-based authentication is where a subset of a department carries out a subset of duties.

27. Answer: b and e
Concept: Password history is the number of passwords you need to use before you can reuse a password. Complex passwords require choosing three from uppercase, lowercase, numbers, and special characters not used in programming. These are harder to guess.

28. Answer: d
Concept: Group policy is used to create password policies for the domain. An example of this is we could use a group policy to prevent users from inserting removable media.

29. Answer: b and e
Concept: Both RADIUS (Microsoft) and TACACS+ (CISCO) are AAA servers.

30. Answer: b
Concept: A proximity card can either be placed on the front of the card reader or swiped to gain access.

31. Answer: e
Concept: NTLM is subject to pass the hash attacks and the passwords are stored as hash values. The BEST way to prevent this attack is to enable Kerberos.

32. Answer: a
Concept: Kerberos uses tickets for authentication in a Microsoft domain environment.

33. Answer: d
Concept: RADIUS is a Microsoft AAA server that uses an Active Directory domain controller to enforce access to the network.

34. Answer: b and c
Concept: Single sign-on is where a user only needs one set of credentials during his session to access files, email, and other domain resources. Both Kerberos and federation use SSO.

35. Answer: a and c
Concept: When a user logs into a system, they are asked to identify themselves; they can do this by inserting a smart card or entering a username.

36. Answer: d
Concept: If the company had an on-boarding policy, it would state that remote workers should have their laptops scanned by the IT team before connecting them to the network.

37. Answer: c
Concept: Although outside of the syllabus, if we use random generated passwords to gain access to a system that held trade secrets, it would be more secure than the others. This appears may appear in the exam.

38. Answer: c
Concepts: The first stage is where a user is identified by using a smart card or username. The second phase is authentication by inserting a password or a PIN, then authorization takes place; this is where a user obtains their access rights.

39. Answer: b and e

Concept: After the identification stage, the authentication stage is next, where a user must insert credentials to prove who they are, for example, with a smart card, by insert a PIN or with a username, inserting a password. After these two stages are complete, the authorization stage kicks in where the user is given access to resources based on their account.

40. Answer: c

Concepts: RADIUS accounting logs statistical data, for example, when a user logs in and when they log out. This data is sometimes used for billing purposes. For exam purposes, they log and track users.

41. Answer: b

Concept: Rule-based authentication is applying to a whole department or a whole category of users.

42. Answer: c

Concept: OpenID Connect uses a third-party method of authentication that sits on top of the OAuth protocol; this could be your Facebook, Google, or Hotmail accounts.

43. Answer: b

Concept: Credential manager is a vault on a computer for storing passwords that use web credentials or Windows accounts.

44. Answer: d

Concept: A periodic permissions audit and review will ensure that old accounts have been deleted and that users do not have the incorrect level of access.

45. Answer: d

Concept: CAC cards are used by the military, PIV is used by federal employees, and smart cards are used by civilians.

46. Answer: d

Concept: With Linux permissions, the first three dashes are the owner, so an owner with full control would be `rwx --- ---` or 7 - -. The middle permissions are for the group, therefore, `--- rwx ---` or -7- is full control. The third group is other or user, therefore, `--- --- rwx` or - - 7 is full control for the user. Setting up least privilege means to give the user the most restricted, therefore, `--- --- r`—gives each user read permissions, hence least privilege has been served.

47. Answer: d

Concept: **False Rejection Rate (FRR)** is where the biometric system will refuse an access attempt by an authorized user.

48. Answer: c and d
Concept: When someone leaves a company, they could have been working on projects with customers, therefore, disabling the account and resetting the password is the best option. They may need to keep the account for a month afterward so the correspondence can be transferred to another employee.

49. Answer: b
Concept: Account lockout will stop brute force but the question asks what will increase the compute time. If I had a three-character complex password, it won't take long to crack. But the longer the password, the more possible permutations there can be, therefore, it is the best choice to use.

50. Answer: d
Concept: A smart card is something you have; you then insert it into a reader that is something you do, and when you enter the PIN, it is something you know.

Chapter 5: Cryptography and PKI Practice Tests

Practice Test 17 – Solution

1. Encryption takes plaintext and turns it into unreadable ciphertext.

2. A wildcard certificate can be used on multiple servers in the same domain. Therefore, when you install it, the name of the server will be inserted into the X509.

3. The old private key is required to decrypt the data. Keys work in pairs and the old public key encrypted the data, therefore, he needs the corresponding private key to decrypt it.

4. A digital signature provides non-repudiation and integrity of the email. He needs to sign it with his private key. There is only one private key.

5. A digital signature provides both integrity, so you know that it has not been tampered with, and non-repudiation as it was signed using the one and only private key.

6. The best form of encryption for small mobile devices is to use **Elliptic Curve Cryptography** (**ECC**) as it has a small footprint and uses the Diffie Hellman handshake.

7. ECC is never used on a military mobile device, instead, AES-256 is used.

8. The two main key stretching algorithms are BCRYPT and PDKDF2.

9. The **Object Identifier** (**OID**) is the equivalent of a serial number embedded into the certificate.

10. The Hardware Security Module is used by the Key Escrow to securely store and manage the private keys. It can also be used with a laptop instead of using a TPM chip for FDE.

11. A key stretching algorithm appends random characters to a stored password; this prevents the storage of duplicate passwords and with additional characters, it will slow down a brute force attack.

12. Hashing is a technique that is used to confirm the integrity of data. The data is hashed, producing a hash value; if the same data is hashed at a later stage and the hash values match, you then know that the integrity of the data is intact. Otherwise, it has been tampered with.

13. The only way to protect data in transit between two entities is to use encryption; this way, the data cannot be viewed or tampered with.

14. Hashing provides data integrity; the two hashing algorithms used on the Security+ exam are SHA1 – 160 bits and MD5 – 128 bits.

15. You should tell the CEO that hashing is a one-way function and it not reversible.

16. A POODLE attack is a man-in-the-middle attack that uses a downgraded version of SSL 3.0 using CBC. Today, we use TLS, which is more secure.

17. DHE and ECDHE are called ephemeral keys; these are short-lived one-time use keys. A new key is used for each session.

18. To protect data on a laptop, we are going to use full disk encryption where the whole drive is encrypted. The laptop will need either a TPM chip or an HSM. Outside of the Security+ exam, an example would be BitLocker, but in the exam, it is known as FDE.

19. To protect data at rest on a mobile telephone, we are going to use **Elliptic Curve Cryptography** (**ECC**). It has a small footprint and is great for small devices.

20. The data stored on a backend server is stored on a database such as SQL or Oracle. This would, therefore, use database encryption.

21. The key that the **Certificate Authority** (**CA**) uses is known as the root key; the CA uses this key to sign the new X509 certificates.

22. When a company does not want to use a third-party external CA, it will use an internal CA using private certificates. The downside of this is that the company needs to build the certificate server and have the in-house skillset to manage it.

23. You would need to implement full device encryption to protect the data on small devices such as smartphones and external or USB drives. The abbreviation for it is FDE.

24. If your company is selling goods to external businesses, they must purchase their certificates from a third-party CA. These are trusted by everyone.

25. If your company is handling military or confidential data, the CA will only be powered up for the issue of new certificates, otherwise, it is powered down and locked up in a secure room to prevent an attack on it.

26. The person who designs and builds the CA and the intermediary authorities is known as the architect.

27. The cyber team should use certificate pinning, which is used to prevent compromise of a CA or someone creating fraudulent certificates.

28. In a Public Key Infrastructure, the CA is responsible for signing the X509 certificates using the root key.

29. When two PKI environments want to trust each other, this is called a bridge of trust model; in the Security+ exam, it is simply known as a trust model.

30. PGP uses a web of trust model and it is used between two people.

31. When FDE is being used and the keys are stored in either a TPM chip or an HSM, it is known as a hardware root of trust model.

32. You should tell him that the validity of certificates is done by the **Certificate Revocation List** (**CRL**). If you do not have internet, you would most probably have a local CRL.

33. If certificate validation is going slow, it means that the CRL is struggling; in this case, you would use a more modern and faster version called the OCSP.

34. Certificate stapling is where a web server bypasses the CRL and goes directly to the OCSP for faster certificate validation.

35. The process for renewing a certificate is called a Certificate Signing Request. Two keys are generated, the public key is sent away, and an X509 certificate is returned.

36. The Key Escrow is responsible for holding the private keys for third-parties. The Key Escrow stores the certificates in an HSM. The HSM secures and manages the certificates.

37. Symmetric encryption such as DES, 3 DES, AES, Twofish, and Blowfish have small single keys known as the private or shared keys. They use block ciphers so that they can encrypt a large amount of data very quickly.

38. When someone's private key has become corrupt, they cannot decrypt data. The DRA then obtains another copy of the private key from the Key Escrow so that they can decrypt the data.

39. A private key is easily identified as it has a P12 format and has a `.pfx` extension. It looks like a certificate being placed inside an envelope. It is the only key protected by a password.

40. A public key is easily identified as it has a P7B format and has a `.cer` extension. It looks like a picture of a certificate. It cannot be protected by a password.

41. Extended validation has a higher level of trust than a normal certificate. When someone visits a website that has this certificate, either the background or the URL letters turn green depending on the browser used.

42. Diffie Hellman is an asymmetric technique that sets up the secure tunnel for the L2TP/IPSec VPN. It does not encrypt data; this is done by the ESP encryption algorithms.

43. A SAN certificate can be installed on multiple domains, you can also add the DNS server or IP Address into the certificate.

44. When the developer has written new software, it should be code signed to prove that it is the original software and not a fake.

45. Block ciphers put data in blocks and stream cipher the data is transferred in bits, therefore, encrypting data using block ciphers is much quicker.

46. L2TP/IPSec has three encryption algorithms in the ESP. These are DES 56 bit, 3DES 168 bit, and AES 256 bit. The strongest is AES and the weakest is DES. The smaller the key, the faster it is, but the larger the key, the more secure it is.

47. The first stage of any encryption in the Security+ exam, whether it is asymmetric or symmetric encryption is to exchange keys.

48. When Bill is encrypting data to send to Ben, he should have first of all, already exchanged public keys. Therefore, Bill will use Ben's public key to encrypt the data.

49. James and Ben must first of all have a key pair as PGP is asymmetric then they should then exchange public keys.

50. To be able to set up PGP, each person needs a key pair.

51. When a certificate is giving an untrusted error, the certificate should be checked to ensure that it has not expired, and if it is valid, then we need to ensure it is added to the Trusted Root Certification Authorities on the computer where the certificate is installed.

52. The CEO and CFO need to digitally sign the email using their private key to ensure that the email has not been tampered with. S/MIME could be used between two people.

53. To protect an email and provide integrity, we would first of all, we would digitally sign the email and to prevent the email from being read in transit, we would then encrypt it.

54. The five symmetric encryption algorithms used in the Security+ exam are DES, 3DES, AES, Blowfish, and Twofish.

55. The only key that is transmitted is a public key; the private key is never exchanged.

56. The only VPN that will use a SSL certificate would be the legacy SSL VPN.

57. Steganography is where data is hidden inside other data; therefore, the packet is larger than expected.

58. Obfuscation is a technique that obscures that format of data so that it cannot be read.

59. Blowfish is faster than Twofish as Blowfish has a 64-bit key whereas Twofish has a 128-bit key. Twofish is, therefore, more secure.

60. When Jane encrypted the data, she used Debra's public key; Debra would then have decrypted the data with her own private key. When replying back to Jane, she would encrypt the reply with Jane's public key, therefore, Jane would have needed to decrypt with her private key, not Debra's public key.

Practice Test 18 – Solution

1. Shorter, secure
2. Salting, appended
3. Laptop, mobile telephone
4. ECC, AES-256
5. Short, ECDHE, DHE
6. Exchange keys
7. PGP
8. Hashing, SHA1, MD5
9. BCRYPT, PBKDF2, compute
10. Integrity, authentication
11. AES, DES, one

12. Private key, shared key
13. Faster, 64, 128
14. Public, private
15. Obfuscation
16. Stateful, steganography
17. Digital signature, private
18. Private, Key Escrow
19. Stapling, OCSP
20. P12, `.pfx`, P7B, `.cer`
21. Pinning
22. Intermediary
23. Hardware Security Module
24. Certificate chain
25. Collision attack

26. 802.1x, RADIUS
27. Certificate Revocation List (CRL), OCSP
28. Wildcard
29. SAN
30. Trust model
31. WPA2-CCMP
32. OID
33. WPS. Password
34. EAP-TLS
35. EAP-TTLS
36. Someone else's private
37. Private, public, private
38. P12, password
39. CER, cannot
40. BASE64
41. Diffusion
42. TLS
43. Symmetric, block
44. Diffie Hellman, IKE
45. DES, 3DES, AES, Twofish
46. Digital Signature, Hashing
47. Self-signed
48. ROT13, 13th, alphabet
49. Nonce
50. Confusion

Practice Test 19 – Solution

Description	Answer
Encrypts large amounts of data	Symmetric encryption
Asymmetric encryption algorithm	RSA
Encryption for data-in-transit	FDE
Key Escrow holds these for third parties	Private keys
Appends random characters to passwords	Salt
Encrypts data at rest	FDE
Strongest VPN encryption	AES
PKI encryption key	Public key
Matching two hashes	Collision
Prevents someone from reading code	Obfuscation
List of precomputed hashes	Rainbow table
Web server bypassing the CRL and going direct to the OCSP	Certificate stapling
A short-lived key	Ephemeral
Used for encrypted data in transit	TLS
Key stretching algorithms, select two	Bcrypt, PBKDF2
Private key is a P12 format, `.pfx` extension protected by a...	Password
Stage 1 when building a CA, you need to choose between	Public or private, CA
Prevent CA compromise and creation of fraudulent certificates	Certificate pinning
Hashing algorithm	MD5
Where the certificate serial number is located	OID
Make an application for a new certificate	CSR
Creates a secure session for a L2TP/IPSec VPN	Diffie Hellman
Check certificate validity when you have no internet	CRL
Certificate that can be used for multiple hosts, same domain	Wildcard
Certificate that can be used across multiple domains and have details such as the IP address inserted	SAN certificate

Practice Test 20 – Mock Exam 5 – Solution

1. Answer: d
Concept: EAP-TLS is wireless authentication where the certificate is installed on the endpoint. EAP-TTLS the certificate is installed on the server.

2. Answer: a

Concept: When you clear the SSL cache, you are clearing the certificate cache and the certificate will no longer be stored on the Trusted Root Certification Authorities on the laptop, hence giving trust errors.

3. Answer: b

Concept: PSK normally uses a password to connect to a wireless access point, but the administrator account for the wireless access point uses a unique username and password.

4. Answer: b

Concept: A Key Escrow holds the private keys for third parties.

5. Answer: b

Concept: 802.1x authenticates users and devices by a certificate.

6. Answer: d

Concept: The CA signs the certificates, but the intermediary authorities issues the certificates.

7. Answer: d

Concept: A self-signed certificate that can be used internally cannot be validated as it has no CRL.

8. Answer: c

Concept: When encrypting and decrypting data, you will use a key pair—the public key to encrypt and the private key to decrypt. Once you update your smart card, a new key pair is issued and these keys can only encrypt and decrypt data moving forward.

9. Answer: c

Concept: When setting up WPS, for example, on a gaming console, you enter a password. After that you invoke the password by pushing a button to gain a wireless connection. Due to the password being stored on the console, it can be subjected to a brute force attack.

10. Answer: a and d

Concept: PGP does not use PKI but each person might provide a key pair. As with any other method of encryption, the first stage in encryption is to exchange keys. Public keys are used to encrypt data and the corresponding private key decrypts the data.

11. Answer: d

Concept: When two different PKIs trust each other, this is known as a bridge of trust, but the CompTIA exam sometimes calls it a trust model.

12. Answer: b and e
Concept: WPA2-Enterprise is a domain-wide wireless authentication that requires a RADIUS server with an 802.1x managed switch as a RADIUS client.

13. Answer: c
Concept: PEM is a Base64 format, CER is a P7B format, and a PFX is a P12 format.

14. Answer: e
Concept: Third party to third party authentication using SAML and extended attributes is federation services. When the connection method changes to a wireless connection, it becomes RADIUS federation.

15. Answer: c
Concept: Certificate pinning prevents fraudulent certificates from being created and prevents CA compromise. It also prevents SSL man-in-the-middle attacks.

16. Answer: c
Concept: Extended validation requires a higher level of trust. When the certificate is installed, the background goes green or in some browsers, the URL goes green.

17. Answer: b
Concept: A public key has a `.cer` extension and a format of P7B.

18. Answer: e, f, and g
Concept: Symmetric encryption uses one key called the private key or shared key. The five symmetric types of encryption are DES, 3DES, AES, Blowfish, and Twofish.

19. Answer: c
Concept: Extended validation certificates provide a higher level of trusted and either turn the background green or the URL letters are green, depending on the browser.

20. Answer: b
Concept: EAP-FAST does not use a certificate and provides mutual authentication. EAP-TLS needs a certificate on the endpoint, EAP-TTLS a certificate on the server, and PEAP uses a certificate for TLS encryption.

21. Answer: b and d
Concept: Ephemeral keys are a one-time use key and these are **Diffie Hellman Ephemeral (DHE)** and **Elliptic Curve Diffie Hellman Ephemeral (ECDHE)**.

22. Answer: d
Concept: The root key is the name of the key used by the CA.

23. Answer: b
Concept: Certificate stapling is where the web server bypasses the CRL for faster lookup.

24. Answer: b
Concept: The **Object Identifier** (**OID**) is where the certificate serial number is located.

25. Answer: d
Concept: Rainbow tables are a list of precomputed passwords with their associated hashes. These can be used to carry out a collision attack where the password hash is being matched.

26. Answer: d
Concept: The certificate chain should have three levels; the middle level shows the CA where the certificate can be validated. The certificate chaining needs three layers; if there are less than this, it would provide a non-trusted certificate error.

27. Answer: c
Concept: L2TP/IPSec uses IPSec in tunnel mode as it encrypts both the AH and the ESP. Diffie Hellman uses IKE to set this tunnel up.

28. Answer: b
Concept: Once a certificate has been compromised, it must be revoked; this will add the certificate to the CRL, preventing it from being used.

29. Answer: d
Concept: When purchasing a new wireless access point, you must purchase the latest most secure models.

30. Answer: b
Concept: A SSL certificate can only be used to set up a legacy SSL VPN, although this would be inadvisable.

31. Answer: b
Concept: Obfuscation is used to mask data and source code so that if it is stolen, it cannot be read.

32. Answer: b and c
Concept: Bcrypt and PBKDF2 can both be used for key stretching; this increases the size of the stored password, making it more difficult to crack the password.

33. Answer: c
Concept: Digitally signed email between two people can be done using S/MIME.

34. Answers: b and d
Concept: Hashing is used for the integrity of data. The two hashing algorithms are SHA1 160-bit and MD5 128-bit. SHA1 has the highest number of bits, making it more secure, whereas MD5 is the fastest.

35. Answer: a
Concept: Salting is a technique where a random value is appended to the passwords being stored that will make duplicate passwords unique.

36. Answer: a
Concept: Email between mail servers can be classified as data in transit and in the CompTIA Security+ exam, they use TLS. In the real world, SMTPS would be used but it is outside the scope of the syllabus.

37. Answer: d
Concept: A wildcard can be used on multiple servers within the same domain and, when installed, the server's name will be installed.

38. Answer: c
Concept: Data in transit is protected by the most secure version TLS. The legacy version that is less secure is SSL.

39. Answer: c
Concept: Encryption between two people can be carried out using PGP.

40. Answer: d
Concept: Before you install a certificate on a laptop or any other device, you need to complete a **Certificate Signing Request** (**CSR**) requesting a new certificate.

41. Answer: a and c
Concept: Visitors need no authentication so they will use open system authentication; however, the employees will need WPA2-Enterprise, which supports domain authentication.

42. Answer: c, e, and f
Concept: Data is decrypted by the Data Recovery Agent using the users private key. The private keys are held by the Key Escrow.

43. Answer: b
Concept: When you connect to the airport wireless access point, you are immediately put into a captive portal where you can accept the free Wi-Fi by entering your details, purchase the premium Wi-Fi, or authenticate yourself using your Facebook account.

44. Answer: b and d
Concept: Bcrypt and PBKDF2 are tools used for key stretching.

45. Answer: d
Concept: He is typing in passwords and then hashing so that he can match the hash of passwords that he has already stolen. This is called a collision attack if he finds a matching hash.

46. Answer: b and e
Concept: A private key has a `.pfx` extension with a format of P12.

47. Answer: a
Concept: A **Subject Alternate Name** (**SAN**) certificate can be used when you need to add multiple domain names, IP addresses, or a DNS Server addresses into the certificate.

48. Answer: c
Concept: Symmetric encryption has a small fast key that encrypt data using block ciphers, making it the perfect choice to encrypt large amounts of data.

49. Answer: b and d
Concept: To protect data at rest, you will need full disk or full device encryption. The laptop will need a TPM chip to store the encryption keys. An example of this would be BitLocker.

50. Answer: d
Concept: Encryption between hosts in the local LAN should use IPSec in transport mode where only the ESP is encrypted.

Chapter 6: Risk Management

Practice Test 21 – Solution

1. The auditor is measuring the Recovery Point Objective, the amount of downtime a company can endure without causing damage to its sales or reputation.

2. The IT manager has been measuring the **Mean Time Between Failures** (**MTBF**) so that he can see, over a period of time, the number of times the video-conferencing application has been crashing. This measures the reliability.

3. The **Mean Time to Repair** (**MTTR**) lets you know how long it took a system to be repaired and the **Recovery Time Objective** (**RTO**) is when a system is back to operational state; they both inform you when the system is working.

4. The quality of how the risk is measured by the Qualitative Risk Assessment can be graded as high, medium, or low.

5. The Quantitative Risk Assessment is normally measured by giving the risk a value to measure the risk.

6. This is known as a single point of failure, where one component fails and takes down a system.

7. The most critical factor measuring Business Impact Analysis is the loss of life.

8. When employing someone, the human resources department must carry out a background check to ensure that they are who they say they are and they have no criminal record. For finance positions, they will also credit check them.

9. An exit interview is carried out by the human resources department to discover the reason why an employee leaves and to see how they can improve working conditions to ensure that they retain good employees.

10. A business partnership agreement lays out the contributions of each partner, which partner will make certain decisions so that they both know where they stand who decides which decisions so that they both know where they stand.

11. A service level agreement is needed for printer maintenance. This is measured in metrics, for example, did they meet the agreement 99% of the time.

12. When you outsource the maintenance of your printers this is called risk transference.

13. A MOU is more than a gentleman's agreement, but a MOA is legally binding.

14. The first stage in risk assessment is to classify the asset; this will then determine how it is handled, stored, and protected. Just think how differently you would treat gold from trash.

15. The first stage the financial director should do is to enforce mandatory vacations and send Mary on holiday. At that time, the financial consultant can log in to her system and have a thorough investigation.

16. They are adopting a clean desk policy, where they clear all paper from their desks. It should really be called a clear desk policy as nobody is interested in how clean the desk is.

17. **Mandatory Access Control** (**MAC**) is based on the classification of the data; the only person who really knows the classification is the data owner, the person who wrote the document.

18. A data custodian is responsible for storing and backing up of data; he is not authorized to give anyone access to it.

19. A contractor who is a member of the IT team such as a service technician would need either an administrative or privileged account.

20. Prior to starting penetration testing, the tester must establish what he should do when he discovers a vulnerability: does he just report it or exploit it as far as he can go?

21. When Ariadne brought her personal laptop into the company, the IT team should have carried out the on boarding policy and at that point, the virus would have been discovered.

22. A job rotation policy is aimed at, first of all, training staff and then discovering whether fraud or theft has occurred.

23. The cashier is not allowed to carry out the whole transaction herself without the Financial Director, which means that they are adopting separation of duties where no one person can carry out the whole transaction.

24. Each department head should document any risk that affects their department and how the risk should be treated. This should be reviewed annually.

25. When the risk seems too high, we would treat it with risk avoidance.

26. Outsourcing the Skype environment to a third party is known as risk transference.

27. Two technical controls that would be used to mitigate risk on a new laptop would be to activate the host-based firewall and install an antivirus solution.

28. The IT manager is adopting risk acceptance as there are rarely (if any) hurricanes and tornadoes in Scotland. This risk is deemed extremely low.

29. He will either write a new policy for the new technology or complete change management on the existing policy.

30. A standard operating procedure is where a company takes a task that needs to be carried out and sets out step-by-step instructions on how to carry out that task and by whom.

31. The purpose of using SLE, ARO, and ALE is to put a monetary value on items that are lost. SLE is the value of losing one item, the ARO is the number of losses a year, and the ALE, the annual loss, is when both of these are multiplied. As long as you have two values, the other can be calculated. For example, *SLE x ARO = ALE* or *ALE /ARO = SLE*.

32. When John Smith began employment, he would have been given the acceptable use policy on using email. In the policy, it would have been stipulated that company email cannot be used for personal email. By sending out this email, he has violated the AUP.

33. Before the forensic investigator starts to analyze the laptop, he must take a system image and place it on another computer, keeping the original intact so that it can be produced in court. Secondly, on the system image, he should hash the data prior to his investigation and then re-hash it at the end and when both values match, he can prove to the judge that the data has not been tampered with.

34. Before the forensic investigator starts to analyze an external hard drive, he must take a forensic copy then place it on another computer, keeping the original intact so that it can be produced in court. He would also hash the data before and after to prove integrity.

35. The chain of custody documents who has collected evidence and who has handled it until it is produced in court as evidence. Once the evidence has left the sight of the personnel who last signed for it, the chain of custody has been broken.

36. His mailbox should be placed on legal hold sometimes called Litigation Hold; this will then mean emails can be sent and received, but cannot be deleted or destroyed and then can be presented as evidence.

37. The first stage of discovering a web-based attack would be to capture the network traffic to identify the attacker as this is the most volatile evidence. Simply stopping the attack stops you from finding out who the perpetrator is.

38. If a rapidly expanding virus is attacking your company network, you need to immediately stop the attack. The time taken to capture the network traffic would allow the virus to be spread all over your network. This is the only case when you must stop it from spreading rather than capture the volatile evidence.

39. When the security administrator discovers that one of the company computers is a member of a botnet, it should be turned off immediately, taken from the network, and re-imaged; this is to prevent it from attacking anyone else. He then should investigate how it happened to prevent another occurrence.

40. The record time offset is the regional time that evidence has been collected. In the case of multinational investigations, it then can put into a sequence with evidence collected in other countries using time normalization. All times may be converted into GMT so a trail of evidence can be established.

41. A snapshot can be taken before a major upgrade so that if the upgrade fails the virtual machine can be rolled back to the original state. The CompTIA exam measures a snapshot as the fastest backup, when in fact, it should be deemed the fastest recovery.

42. The fastest physical backup is a full backup. A full backup is the last full backup, but both incremental and differential backups start with a full backup then replay the differential or the number of incremental backups required.

43. The most expensive disaster recovery site is a hot site as it is fully manned and operation with data with the data up to date.

44. The cheapest disaster recovery site is a cold site as it only has power and water and no equipment.

45. Data sovereignty means that data cannot be stored outside of the region it was created in. In the exam it could also mean country, data must reside within the country where it was created.

46. If your company is backing up data using backup tapes, they must ensure that the tapes are clearly labeled and that the latest backup is taken offsite.

47. For a business selling theater tickets, they must use a hot site for disaster recovery.

48. A cloud-based disaster recovery site can be up and running faster than any other site because all you need is an internal connection; even with a hot site, a company needs to move all of the people to that hot site and that may take some time.

49. A cold site would be the cheapest disaster recovery site as it would only have power and water. There would be no equipment and it may take some time to become operational.

50. Risk is the probability that an event will happen that would cause some loss to the company.

Practice Test 22 – Solution

1. Data owner
2. Deterrents
3. Compensating

4. Clean desk policy
5. Background, credit checks
6. Mandatory vacations, job rotation
7. Standard operation procedures
8. Business Impact Analysis
9. Off-boarding, exit interviews
10. Non-disclosure agreement
11. Recovery Point Objective, Recovery Time Objective
12. Mean time between failures
13. Increase, decrease
14. Separation of duties
15. Risk acceptance
16. Risk avoidance
17. Risk mitigation, technical
18. Single point of failure
19. Service level agreement
20. Interconnection security agreement
21. Not legally, agreement
22. Business partnership agreement
23. Detective
24. Residual risk
25. Shred, pulverizing
26. Confidential
27. Data Loss Prevention
28. Pulping

29. Classified, destruction certificate
30. Acceptable use policy
31. Acceptable use policy, on-boarding policy
32. Rules of behavior
33. Environmental
34. Nation state
35. Script kiddie
36. Single loss expectancy, annual rate of occurrence
37. Identify, asset
38. Risk register, treatment
39. Risk mitigation
40. Risk transference
41. Change management
42. Tabletop exercise
43. Hot, cold

44. Data classification
45. Shredding, pulverization, degaussing
46. Competitor
47. Mission critical
48. Lessons learned
49. Order of volatility
50. Recovery procedures

Practice Test 23 – Solution

Description	Answer
An agreement more than a gentleman's agreement but not legally binding	MOU
Risk treatment—risk too high	Avoidance
When a system has been returned to an operational state	RTO
Using a username and password when your smart card expires	Compensating control
How long it takes to repair a system	MTTR
The first stage after finding a remote attack	Capture network traffic
Used when the auditor has been to visit and finds adverse actions, select two	Shredding, pulverizing
Risk treatment—outsourcing	Transference
After taking a system image, next stage	Hash the data
Number of events per year	ARO
How evidence should be controlled	Chain of custody
Risk—calculating loss	Quantitative
Loss of a single item	SLE
Fastest physical backup	Full
Amount of time a system can be down without impacting the business	RPO
Fastest backup	Snapshot
Risk treatment—risk very low	Acceptance
After identifying a virus, the next stage, choose two	Quarantine, Isolate
SLE X ARO	ALE
Best way to dispose of paper	Pulping
Risk—high, medium, or low	Qualitative

What you will do with the record time offset	Time normalization
Two ways to dispose of a hard drive	Shredding, pulverizing
Prevent data from being deleted	Legal hold
Risk treatment—technical control to reduce risk	Mitigation

Practice Test 24 – Mock Exam 6 – Solution

1. Answer: d
Concept: By using mandatory vacations, the expert can look through the suspects desk and local files on the computer as well as the company files and he will not be restricted in his investigations.

2. Answer: d
Concept: When someone writes a policy, fills out a form, or conducts change management, then this is an administrative control. Watch out for the word policy. Least privilege is not a control.

3. Answer: a
Concept: An intrusive scan is going into the system similar to pen testing and can cause damage.

4. Answer: c
Concept: Classified paper waste is put into burning bags and incinerated by a contractor who will provide a destruction certificate.

5. Answer: b and c
Concept: SIEM systems monitor events using a separate input filter on each. They must be monitoring the correct type of host too.

6. Answer: c
Concept: A white box penetration tester has all of the knowledge of the application and can use a technique known as fuzzing that puts random information into an application to test for vulnerabilities.

7. Answer: e
Concept: A nation state is a foreign government that is very well organized and funded.

8. Answer: c
Concept: Quantitive risk is a measure as a numerical value against a particular hazard.

9. Answer: d
Concept: Record time offset is the regional time that evidence is collected. After the times have been taken across all of the countries, you will then adopt time normalization. For example, you may convert all of the times into GMT then Interpol will be able to trace where the flow of data starts and finishes.

10. Answer: a and c
Concept: Think of the auditor as the snitch; he will not stop anything from happening. His job is to inform management of things going wrong and his recommendations to improve the situation. Auditors will audit many things but need the policies and procedures to ensure that the company is compliant—without these, he has nothing to measure against.

11. Answer: b, c, e, and f
Concept: FDE encrypts the data at rest but not in transit. A MDM is a centrally managed solution that can ensure that the mobile devices are fully hardened and remote wiped if lost or stolen

12. Answer: b and c
Concept: Both are formal agreements between two parties, but only the MOA is a legally binding document.

13. Answer: c and d
Concept: MTTR shows the time it would take to repair a system and the MTBF shows how reliant the system is.

14. Answer: c
Concept: When a remote or web-based attack is discovered, you must capture the network traffic so that the culprit can be identified and prosecuted.

15. Answer: a
Concept: Chain of custody shows who has handled the evidence, but when the evidence was placed in the hold, the chain was broken.

16. Answer: a
Concept: Lessons learned is a detective control that will examine the facts about an incident to prevent reoccurrence.

17. Answer: c and d
Concept: A computer needs to have a system image captured so it can be investigated on another computer. A hard drive has no GUI therefore a forensic copy will be taken.

18. Answer: b
Concept: When analyzing the BIA, we need to look first of all at the RPO, the amount of time a company can sustain without its data, sometimes measured as acceptable downtime. Secondly, they would look at the RTO when the company return to an operational state.

19. Answer: d
Concept: A gray box pen tester has at least one piece of information prior to start testing.

20. Answer: a
Concept: If we think of credentialed as having admin rights, the credentialed intrusive will cause more damage than just a normal intrusive scan.

21. Answer: a, c, and e
Concept: A hot site is manned and data is replicated immediately making it the most expensive to run. A warm site is manned and up and running with data 3-4 hours old. The cold site is the cheapest as it is not manned and has no equipment.

22. Answer: d
Concept: Single point of failure is where a single component stops a system. In this case, it prevented an aircraft from flying.

23. Answers: a and c
Concepts: A Faraday cage acts like a force field stop data emission and prevents a remote attacker from accessing data.

24. Answer: a
Concept: Qualitative risk evaluates the risk as high, medium, or low assessment.

25. Answer: b
Concept: Military contracts require a supply chain assessment to ensure they can fulfill the contact and have good quality products. Otherwise, it makes the military vulnerable.

26. Answer: b
Concept: The best way to dispose of paper waste is burning, then pulping, and shredding, in that order.

27. Answer: c
Concept: A competitor is the most likely to steal your trade secrets so that he can get your new product to market before you.

28. Answer: a, d
Concept: On-boarding are checks that are done before a device is attached to the network. AUP lets the user know what they can and cannot do with a piece of equipment.

29. Answer: a
Concept: The first stage in risk assessment is to identify or classify the asset. This classification determines its value and how it should be handled or treated.

30. Answer: a
Concept: When destroying hard drives, the best way is to shred the hard drive—some turn the hard drive into powder. The next best is to pulverize followed by degaussing.

31. Answer: b and d
Concept: The ARO is calculated by dividing the ALE by the SLE. The ALE is calculated by multiplying the SLE/ARO.

32. Answer: c
Concept: Job rotation has two purposes—the first is to ensure that all staff can perform more than one job and the second is to help to detect fraud and theft. If they had adopted job rotation, someone else would have had experience of being a mail administrator.

33. Answer: b and c
Concept: A risk register includes all of the company's risk, a risk owner, the value of the asset, and the risk treatment.

34. Answer: d
Concept: A mantrap is a turnstile type device that only allows one person to enter or leave the data center, making it a safe and contained environment. The exam likes protecting a data center by using a mantrap.

35. Answer: b
Concept: All scans will show details of the host and the date/time of the scan. A normal vulnerability scan will find missing patches. These are known as passive, also non-credentialed has minimal rights. Whenever passive and non-credentialed are in the same question, choose the latter.

36. Answer: c
Concept: A hacktivist is politically motivated.

37. Answer: d
Concept: Legal hold on a mailbox prevents the emails from being deleted but allows the person under investigation to still send and receive email.

38. Answer: d
Concept: The dark web is a place where illegal dealing occurs including selling of unauthorized programs and tools that are likely to cause damage.

39. Answer: e
Concept: A new intern is most likely as they are untrained users and the most likely to fall victim to a spear phishing attack.

40. Answer: d
Concept: Pulverizing is a better way to destroy a hard drive than degaussing. Burning and pulping could not be carried out.

41. Answer: d
Concept: A table-top exercise is a hypothetical exercise and is an easy way to walk through a disaster recovery plan.

42. Answer: b
Concept: A full backup is the fastest physical backup. All backups start with a full backup. A snapshot is the fastest restore and has the ability to roll back, but is used in a virtual environment. An incremental backup uses a full back up and the number of incremental tapes since that backup. A differential backup uses the full backup and the latest differential, tape, always using two tapes.

43. Answer: b
Concept: Collecting information from social media websites will be used to target a single person. This is how social engineering is carried out.

44. Answer: c
Concept: A credentialed scan is a passive scan that can provide information from a system and audit files. A non-credentialed and passive scan is limited to missing patches and the IP Address and time of scan. The Microsoft Baseline Analyzer is a credentialed scan.

45. Answer: c
Concept: Replication of data between countries is illegal. Data must stay within regions. In the Security+ exam, it could be countries rather than regions.

46. Answer: d
Concept: Active reconnaissance is where someone has entered a system. In the preceding cases, they had accessed the systems registry and the operating system files.

47. Answer: c
Concept: A compensating control means something different than what is being used.

48. Answer: c
Concept: A DLP template is an XML template with a pattern match inside. When DLP is used, any email matching that pattern match will be blocked. DLP can also be used to prevent data being stolen by USB.

49. Answer: d

Concept: When troubleshooting virus attacks, use the mnemonic IP. I = Identify the virus, then isolate/quarantine. Next is P = Preparation stage – apply a solution – or mitigate (delete). In this preceding example, we have no virus name, therefore, we have not identified it. We would then run a virus scan to identify the virus.

50. Answer: b, c, and f

Answer: Technical controls normally mitigate risk. Antivirus prevents virus attacks, screen saver locks your desktop after a period of time, and firewall rules control what traffic flows in and out of the desktop

Other Books You May Enjoy

If you enjoyed this book, you may be interested in these other books by Packt:

CompTIA Security+ Certification Guide
Ian Neil

ISBN: 978-1-78934-801-9

- Get to grips with security fundamentals from Certificates and Encryption to Identity and Access Management
- Secure devices and applications that are used by your company
- Identify the different types of malware and virus and take appropriate actions to protect against them
- Protect your environment against social engineering and advanced attacks
- Implement PKI concepts
- Learn about secure coding techniques, quality control, and testing
- Troubleshoot common security issues

CompTIA Network+ Certification Guide
Glen D. Singh, Rishi Latchmepersad

ISBN: 978-1-78934-050-1

- Explain the purpose of a variety of networking concepts and implement them appropriately
- Understand physical security and common attacks while securing wired and wireless networks
- Understand the fundamentals of IPv4 and IPv6
- Determine and explain the appropriate cabling, device, and storage technologies
- Understand network troubleshooting methodology and appropriate tools to support connectivity and performance
- Use best practices to manage the network, determine policies, and ensure business continuity

Leave a review - let other readers know what you think

Please share your thoughts on this book with others by leaving a review on the site that you bought it from. If you purchased the book from Amazon, please leave us an honest review on this book's Amazon page. This is vital so that other potential readers can see and use your unbiased opinion to make purchasing decisions, we can understand what our customers think about our products, and our authors can see your feedback on the title that they have worked with Packt to create. It will only take a few minutes of your time, but is valuable to other potential customers, our authors, and Packt. Thank you!

Index

www.ingramcontent.com/pod-product-compliance
Lightning Source LLC
Chambersburg PA
CBHW080636060326
40690CB00021B/4951